The Gift of Knowing:
A Biblical Perspective on Knowing and Truth

2nd Edition

*Volume 1 of God's Gifts for the Christian Life –
Part 1: The Gift of Knowledge*

J. Alexander Rutherford

Unless otherwise indicated, all Scripture quotations are from The Holy Bible, English Standard Version® (ESV®), copyright © 2001 by Crossway Bibles, a publishing ministry of Good News Publishers. Used by permission. All rights reserved.

Unless otherwise indicated, all Scripture quotations from the book of Habakkuk or those marked Teleioteti are my own translations. Translations from Habakkuk are taken from the translation published in my commentary on Habakkuk (Vancouver, Teleioteti 2019).

Paperback ISBN-13: 978-1-989560-23-5
EBook ISBN-13: 978-1-989560-24-2

Copyright © 2021 J. Alexander Rutherford
Teleioteti publishing, Vancouver BC
All rights reserved.

1st Edition, 1st Printing, ©2019
2nd Printing, ©2020

Cover Design: Stephen Joshua Arriola

To contact Teleioteti publishing for information or to provide feedback, please visit us at **https://teleioteti.ca** or email us at **info@teleioteti.ca**.

DEDICATION

This book is dedicated to my Lord and Saviour Jesus Christ; it is my prayer that this little book would magnify your holy name. Also, to my young daughter Aliyah Mercedes Rutherford, I dedicate this book to you, praying that you would commit yourself to Him and find all your hope and joy in the one who gave His life for you.

The secret things belong to the LORD our God, but the things that are revealed belong to us and to our children forever, that we may do all the words of this law. – Deut 29:29

CONTENTS

Dedication iii
Contents v
Analytical Outline vii
Acknowledgments ix
Series Introduction xi
Introduction 1
   1. Diagnosing the Disease 5
Part 1— Our Epistemological Situation 19
   2. Worldview Thinking: Appropriate Subjectivity 21
   3. The Truth is Out There: Appropriate Objectivity 29
Part 2— The Standard of Epistemology 41
   4. A Word from Beyond: Appropriate Authority 43
   5. The Covenantal Revelation of Creation 47
   6. The Covenantal Revelation of God's Speech 57
   7. The Ethics of Knowing 71
Part 3— The Practice of Epistemology 79
   8. Created in the Image of God: Thinking as a Creature 81

9. Created with Senses: Empirical Knowledge 87

10. Created with a Mind: Rational Thought and Logic 93

Conclusion 106

    Glossary 110

    Bibliography 118

    About Teleioteti 122

    Other Books by J. Alexander Rutherford 123

ANALYTICAL OUTLINE

I. INTRODUCTION
   1. CHAPTER 1 – DIAGNOSING THE DISEASE
      a. Pre-Modernity – Autonomy in Pursuit of Universal Truth.
      b. Modernity – Autonomy in Search of Objectivity
      c. Postmodernity – Autonomy Arriving at Radical Relativity

II. PART 1: OUR EPISTEMOLOGICAL SITUATION
   2. CHAPTER 2 – WORLDVIEW THINKING: APPROPRIATE SUBJECTIVITY
      - Excursus: Another Perspective on Subjectivity
   3. CHAPTER 3 – THE TRUTH IS OUT THERE: APPROPRIATE OBJECTIVITY
      a. Showing a Worldview to Be True
      b. Showing a Worldview to be Self-Destructing
      c. Appealing to the Truth Suppressed in Unrighteousness
      - Excursus: Trancendental Arguments

III. PART 2: THE STANDARD OF EPISTEMOLOGY
   4. CHAPTER 4 – A WORD FROM BEYOND: APPROPRIATE AUTHORITY
   5. CHAPTER 5 – THE COVENANTAL REVELATION OF CREATION
      a. Creation Revelation in the Testimony of the Creation
      b. Creation Revelation in the Morality of the Created Order
      c. Creation Revelation in the Human Faculties
      - Excursus: On the Contribution of Objects
   6. CHAPTER 6 – THE COVENANTAL REVELATION OF GOD'S SPEECH

- a. The Authority and Inerrancy of Scripture
- b. The Sufficiency of Scripture
- c. The Clarity of Scripture
7. CHAPTER 7 – THE ETHICS OF KNOWING
    - Excursus: On Reading or the Possibility Thereof

IV. PART 3: THE PRACTICE OF EPISTEMOLOGY
8. CHAPTER 8 – MAN IN THE IMAGE OF GOD: THINKING AS A CREATURE
    - a. God is the Reference Point for Meaning
    - b. We Must Pursue Knowledge in Humility
9. CHAPTER 9 – MAN CREATED WITH SENSES: EMPIRICAL KNOWLEDGE
    - a. The Biblical Affirmation of the Senses
    - b. The Problem with the Senses
    - c. Conclusion
10. CHAPTER 10 – MAN CREATED WITH A MIND: RATIONAL THOUGHT AND LOGIC
    - a. The Presupposition of Thought
    - b. The Necessary Condition of Thought
    - c. The Content of Thought
        - i. Concrete Thought
        - ii. Abstract Thought
    - d. Conclusion

V. CONCLUSION
VI. GLOSSARY

ACKNOWLEDGMENTS

Countless individuals have helped me to think through the issues raised in the book, too many to acknowledge. But among the many voices that have helped shape my thinking about the Scriptures and this world, Brad Copp and John Frame deserve special mention.

I had the pleasure of studying under Brad at Pacific Life Bible College. Brad was the first person who introduced me to the questions of epistemology and pointed me to Scripture as the primary authority for the Christian. It was also Brad who chose to John Frame's *Theology of Lordship* as the valedictorian prize when I graduated from PLBC. It is this series that has had the most formative influence on my thinking. I am deeply indebted to the teaching of John Frame; his faithfulness to the word of God, clarity in communication, and profundity make a rare combination. Anyone familiar with his work will see its influence in what follows.

SERIES INTRODUCTION

> His divine power has granted to us all things that pertain to life and godliness, through the knowledge of him who called us to his own glory and excellence. – 2 Peter 1:3

God has not left his people without help in the day of trouble—or in the day of prosperity for that matter. The Bible is God's gift to his people, revealing to them Jesus Christ and the salvation he has accomplished. But the gift of Scripture does not end in revealing our need for salvation and God's provision for it; Scripture is sufficient for the entire Christian life. In his second epistle, Peter tells us that God's divine power has given us everything for life and godliness (2 Pet 1:3, cf. 2 Tim 3:16-17).

In *God's Gifts for the Christian Life*, J. Alexander Rutherford unpacks how God through the Bible has given us what we need to live faithfully in his world. Each volume unpacks the Scriptural teaching against the background of contemporary culture and shows how the Bible provides a firm foundation for our lives. Each volume is intended to be short, around 110-150 pages, and accessible to the interested reader. The primary audience is theologically interested lay-Christians (Christians who are not in paid ministry and have no formal theological training), students, and pastors.

Part 1, The Gift of Knowledge, will address the questions raised by philosophy and culture concerning the nature and possibility of knowledge and truth. Part 2, The Gift of Truth, will provide an overview of the Bible and its content to equip the reader for a lifelong engagement with Scriptures and with the world Scripturally. Part 3, The Gift of Wisdom, will orient the Christian life towards culture and the church in order to show what it looks like to live a faithful, theological life. Drawing on the resources given in Parts 1 & 2, Part 3 will set forth a framework for Christians to engage intellectually with culture, life, and the local church in order to serve better within the local church context and so further God's purpose in the world.

INTRODUCTION

"What were we doing when we unchained this earth from its sun?" spoke the madman, "Where is it moving to now? Where are we moving to? Away from all suns? Are we not continually falling? And backwards, sidewards, forwards, in all directions? Is there still an up and a down? Aren't we straying as though through an infinite nothing?"[1] Friedrich Nietzsche, an atheist, penned these words more than a century ago, seeing better than any of his peers what atheism would do to the Western world. Does not our world feel like this some days? News story after news story evokes in us the thought that the world truly has gone mad! This madness of our world may be most evident in its rejection of the very possibility of truth

Within Christianity, the trustworthiness of the Bible is ever in question. In the culture around us, long-held moral standards have faced sustained erosion, now giving way to a tide of immorality. Without truth, anything goes; concepts of gender, religion, politics, science, and morality are all up for grabs in the Western world. The effects of the erosion of truth we now witness are not merely concerns for students and academics, philosophers and theologians. They have serious implications for every person. They have serious implications for Christians more than anyone else.

If you have picked this book up, you are probably aware of this problem. I do not hope to offer in the pages that follow anything new or an agenda for

---

[1] This is modernised from Friedrich Wilhelm Nietzsche and Walter Kaufmann, *The Portable Nietzsche* (New York, N.Y.: Penguin Books, 1982), 95.

fixing what is wrong in our society. I hope only to offer an application of the Christian Scriptures to the epistemological conundrum we now face, to the crisis of knowing we are in.[2] I hope to show how God has graciously given us what we need to persevere in and thrive while our culture continues to struggle with the noose it has tied for itself. I intend to argue that our culture has been infected with a virus; it has been afflicted with a disease that has characterized every human culture from the beginning of the creation. This disease is the belief in human autonomy; it is this belief that has eroded the concept of truth in the Western world. I will then argue that the remedy for this crisis is a Biblical epistemology, essentially that knowing is a gift from God, coming from and depending upon him.

Believing that God has given us all things we need in Scripture so that we may be equipped for every good work (2 Tim. 3:16-17), I want to show that the Bible has answers to this crisis. I have endeavoured to demonstrate that the Bible gives important insights into the subject of philosophy often called **epistemology**, a model of what it means to know and how we do so.

This volume is written for the concerned Christian, for those of us who see the problem and yet struggle with an answer. Though we will be dealing with philosophy and philosophers, I will not assume a background in philosophy. I write to those who are concerned with what they see and hear yet cannot quite diagnosis the problem or formulate a response. I will not be able to answer all of your questions. Yet by the Lord's grace, I hope to point you to the treasure trove that is Scripture so that together we can be encouraged in our faith, be driven to the worship of our heavenly Father, and be equipped to submit every thought to obey Christ (2 Cor 10:5).

To these ends, this volume's ten short chapters will diagnose the disease that has infected our culture and then point us to the Biblical remedy. First, we will begin with the diagnosis, tracing the destructive virus from its beginnings. We will then look at what we mean by "knowing," addressing the objectivity and subjectivity of knowledge and the nature of truth. With these pieces in place, we can then consider the heart of the crisis, the question of

---

[2] **Epistemology** is a 50 dollar philosophical word used to describe the study of truth and knowing, the act of attaining truth. Epistemology addresses what we think and how we think it, what truth means and how we can find it—if we can at all. This book is a study in epistemology, a study of what the Bible says about truth and the manner of attaining it.

authority. Finally, we will consider ourselves—human beings—as thinking creatures and how God has equipped us to know the world around us.

It is my earnest prayer that we would each come to see and truly believe that the fear of the Lord is the beginning of wisdom. I offer this book as an attempt to show how Scripture provides us with the anchor we need in the epistemological chaos of our time. To this end, I offer this prayer to the Lord for myself and for you, the reader,

> To you, oh Lord, belong all wisdom, knowledge, and understanding,
>> to you these belong, and to those with whom you share them.
> We ask that you would give us wisdom,
>> wisdom necessary to know you and your world.
> Teach us what it means to know the truth and be set free,
>> to fear you and be endowed with true wisdom.
> Help us take every thought captive to obey Christ
>> and to exult in the rich grace you poured out on your people,
>> in eternal life, to know Jesus Christ and you who sent him.
>
> It is in his name that we pray these things,
> amen.

DIAGNOSING THE DISEASE

> For the wrath of God is revealed from heaven against all ungodliness and unrighteousness of men, who by their unrighteousness suppress the truth. For what can be known about God is plain to them, because God has shown it to them. For although they knew God, they did not honor him as God or give thanks to him, but they became futile in their thinking, and their foolish hearts were darkened. Claiming to be wise, they became fools, and exchanged the glory of the immortal God for images resembling mortal man and birds and animals and creeping things. – Romans 1:18-23

In the beginning, God created, and it was good. Since then, things have gone sideways—and backwards, forwards, in all directions! The problem of truth that confronts us today is a story almost as old as time. In Romans 1:18-32, Paul describes the human condition in dark terms. The wrath of God is against all the unrighteousness of man; none of us escape his sweeping indictment (cf. Rom 3:1-23). What should strike us here is the root of the problem, that which causes all sorts of wretched actions and ideas to pour out of our minds and mouths.

My former pastor Fred Eaton once described the problem as disordered worship, disordered worship producing disordered living. Though God has made himself known clearly in the creation, humanity has exchanged the glorious truth of God's existence and character for a lie. Observe that this fundamental sin is a sin of knowledge. Setting aside the truth of God, humans have adopted a lie. Setting aside the Creator, they have made the creature the measure of truth. All human history is stained by this exchange.

Adam and Eve began this trend when they exchanged the command of God for the lie of the Devil. Did "God actually say," asked the tempter—words all too familiar to us today. In the place of the truth of God's goodness, they believed the lie that they knew what was best for themselves. Believing that lie, they fell headfirst into sin and brought all their progeny with them. Since then, all of humanity has made the same deliberate decision to exchange the truth of who God is and his commands for autonomy, the ability to choose what to believe and what to do.

The people whom God called forth from Egypt, those whom he would use to achieve redemption for the world, were not free from this. After leaving Egypt, their trials in the barren wilderness led the Israelites to forsake the promises of God, to reject his goodness and to yearn for the land from which they left:

> Now the rabble that was among them had a strong craving. And the people of Israel also wept again and said, "Oh that we had meat to eat! We remember the fish we ate in Egypt that cost nothing, the cucumbers, the melons, the leeks, the onions, and the garlic. But now our strength is dried up, and there is nothing at all but this manna to look at." (Num 11:4-6)

This was the response of those who received the oracles of God! The world outside of Israel was no different; it embraced this exchange to a much greater extent. This was seen at every level of culture and society, especially in philosophy.

A. Pre-Modernity – Autonomy in Pursuit of Universal Truth

This is no place to give an account of all Philosophy before the so-called Enlightenment and Modernity. Still, we can see the beginning of our contemporary crisis in two strands of so-called "Pre-modern" thought. Though Philosophy was not the exclusive domain of the Western world (much of the thought identified with Greece had its parallels in India), the West is what has most shaped our society. So we will focus on the philosophers and thought of the Western world.

Philosophy as we know it had its origins in Greece. From the early thinkers known as the "Pre-Socratics" to their (slightly) more famous successors Socrates, Plato, and Aristotle, Greek thought was consumed with the tension between unchanging and changing reality. The Pre-Socratics lived at a time when Greece was highly religious; the religion of the day was the worship of the Olympian gods—Zeus, Athena, Ares, etc. In the city of Miletus, around 600 BC, Western philosophy was born as an effort to explain the nature of the world by human reason without reference to the activity of gods.

Instead of explaining the course of nature (e.g. seasons and storms) with an appeal to the supposed life of the different gods and their conflicts, the first philosophers asked questions about the ultimate nature of the world and sought an explanation for their experience beyond the realm of the ancient religion. In this context, a debate emerged among the 2nd generation of these philosophers concerning whether reality was entirely changing or entirely unchanging.[1]

On the one hand, they had the experience of change: we all experience change in the passing of time, in aging, and in new experiences each day. So Heraclitus (535-475 BC), thought change was the ultimate explanation of everything—all changed! This threatened the very possibility of knowledge—for if everything changes, does "truth" change too? Others argued that if change was real, if our experience was what it seemed to be, knowledge was an illusion. Parmenides, the key thinker on this side, rejected the possibility that knowledge was an illusion and instead argued that all change was an illusion. Nothing changed; therefore, our senses could not be trusted. But our minds could come to some understanding of truth.

Philosophy did not linger here long: the next generation of philosophers—mainly Plato (5th-4th centuries BC) and Aristotle (384-322 BC)—attempted to explain change without dispensing with unchanging reality. The greatest Greek philosophers argued that neither change nor eternity (i.e. unchangingness) made sense of the world and human thoughts and experience. Heraclitus was right to observe that things change, but Parmenides was also right when he argued that we need something unchanging if knowledge is possible. What was necessary was a combination

---

[1] Zeno is (relatively) famous for his paradoxes concerning the impossibility of change. He was audacious enough to claim that in a race, if given a slight head start, a tortoise would beat a hare. The ridiculousness of this scenario supposedly revealed the ridiculousness of change.

of something changing, the stuff we experience (which they called *matter*) and that which was unchanging, the true object of knowledge. They contended that what changes is ultimately unknowable, for what it once was is no longer what it is the next moment.

Imagine yourself, they argued, in a stream. If all the water has already moved downriver after it has touched you, is the water you are currently in the same thing? On one level it is—you are still in the same "stream"—yet if the water has changed and the soil beneath your feet is being worn away, what makes this stream the same from one moment to the next? If you claim to know anything about the stream, it cannot be anything about the matter you experience; this is constantly changing. What you know is something beyond the matter that you experience. Therefore, the true object of knowledge must be unchanging, something beyond the sensible world. The sensible world, therefore, really is not knowable at all. But there is something that we do know. This knowable world must lay behind—or above—the matter we sense.

For Plato, the unchanging objects of human knowledge are the **universals**,[2] eternal ideas that exist beyond the physical world in a separate, intangible world of ideas. If you look out your window and see a tree, the true object of your knowledge, for Plato, is not that particular maple in your front yard. Instead, you know the "treeness" that the tree embodies. "Treeness" is the universal, that thing that all trees have in common. For Plato the nature of a tree, table, or human being is that unchangeable element that every tree, table, or human shares. Treeness is that thing which, if you removed it, would make that tree no longer a tree. It is not colour, for trees have different colours, nor is it size or shape. It is something intangible, inexpressible, which lays behind the variety of our experience. Every tree is merely a particular example of this universal idea, this form; it is an embodiment of an idea in matter, what some philosophers call an instantiation.[3] At this point you may be thinking to yourself, "what does

---

[2] Every word in **bold-text** can be found in the glossary at the end of the book. I only bold the words the first time they occur in a chapter.

[3] Universals can be a difficult concept to wrap our minds around. A universal, for Plato, referred not to specific examples of a tree, but the perfect "tree." By definition, such a tree could not physically exist; it could not exist in the sensible world. Therefore, it could only be an idea, a sort of template by which all other trees take their features. In one illustration, Plato pictured the relationship of

'treeness' have to do with the modern dilemma we are in?" The answer is that the concepts with which Plato wrestled have had a profound impact on Christian and non-Christian thought since he first penned them in his dialogues. We can see the implications of his thought more clearly if we consider morality.

One of the dialogues Plato wrote is called *Euthyphro*, in which he struggled with the question of goodness. He is particularly interested in what makes a particular action good or bad. Was it the gods? We know they disagree, argued Plato, so which one do we trust? If we select the highest of them, what if he changes his mind? The Greek gods were fickle beings who did whatever they wanted for their own benefit—even the "best" of them. If morality depended on their mood and decision, could not Zeus declare rape to be right one day and wrong another? The answer to his initial question—what makes a particular action good or bad—could not be in the changing will of even the most powerful being. The answer must be in something unchanging, in the universal of goodness. The universal of goodness would be that unchanging moral standard that lies behind every declaration that something is good—whether it is a god or a human who proclaims it. If, however, this "goodness" judged even the actions of the gods, it is clear that this "goodness" is the true god—an impersonal standard existing beyond all that is sensible, unchanging and perfect. The gods, then, argued Plato, really are not gods at all.[4] Not all Greek thinkers were so concerned about morality, however. For some, truth was a matter of money.

The Sophists, those who peddled wisdom and clever speech to make a wage, did not care about the truthfulness of what they taught. The Sophists cared for "truth" only as content that they were skilled enough to make

---

universal (treeness) and particular (a tree) with an jar and its shadow. As light shines on a jar and casts a rough copy of it on the wall behind, so the idea of something creates imperfect representations of itself in the material world. In morality, there is the idea of "goodness"; every good act is an imperfect example of ideal goodness.
    If you are still struggling, take comfort. I think these "universals" ultimately do not make sense and are false. You cannot imagine "goodness" apart from good acts because it does not exist apart from them; the same goes for humanness, being, etc. See chapter 10 of this volume and Volume 3, *The Gift of Seeing*.
    [4] Christianity provides an answer to this dilemma. Essentially, God's faithfulness means that He is an unchanging standard of what is good and bad. See chapter 10 and my book *Believe the Unbelievable*, 82-87.

money teaching or for its pragmatic value, its usefulness, for their vision of society. They were relativists. That is, truth or falsehood did not matter; only the subjective value of ideas mattered. Did it work? make them money? achieve their vision? Surely this sounds familiar. For the Sophists, only the ends they wanted to achieve and their jobs as skilled teachers mattered not the truth.

For Plato and those who followed him, we could identify their concern as the **transcendent**: they exchanged the truth of God as revealed in his creation for distant *ideas*, not tangible *things*.[5] Instead of that which they could taste or touch, they sought what could be grasped with the mind. They looked for something greater than themselves, something that explained how humans could think and know right and wrong. With transcendence came **objectivism**, the belief that truth was out there to be grasped, that truth would be the same no matter who thought about it.[6] Yet their transcendent ideas, these ideas that were so far beyond humanity and their world, were not the Biblical God. These ideas were impersonal: they explained human thinking but made no demands upon man. They never called for his submission.

In this, the Sophists with their self-interest and the Platonists with their rational thought shared something in common: humanity was the measure of truth or value. For the Sophists, because no transcendence imposed itself upon them, they were free to pursue whatever it was they valued most—namely, a wage attained through skill and their political ends. For the Platonists, truth was what explained human thinking. It was that which the

---

[5] **Transcendence** is a key idea in philosophy and theology, describing that which is other than man, that which is far off or different. It is basically a spatial concept, referring to something above us, "up there." In philosophy or theology it refers to the quality of being greater than and so exercising control over. The universal ideas are greater than human thoughts, human ideas. They are the true content of human thinking and so exercise control over it.

[6] **Objectivity** is a key concept of modernity, a movement whose effects we still feel. To be objective is to be neutral, to be free from bias: if truth is objective and is attained through objective thinking, it is the exact same no matter who is thinking it. No matter who runs the test, not only should the results be the same but their interpretation as well. Is, for example, a rock red if no one observes that it is red? If so, then "the rock is red" is objective truth, but if "the rock is red" is only true when someone observes that it is red, then it is **subjective** truth.

human mind could conjure up to explain itself and its experience. Having rejected the gods, these latter philosophers sought a firm foundation for human knowledge, an objective reality beyond the mind that would be a sufficient object of human thought. They sought universal truth and thought they found it in the unchanging universals or forms.

The ideas raised by these Greek Philosophers remained influential for the next 2000 years, with many (maybe all) of the most profound philosophers of the following millennia interacting with their ideas. Though it is certainly an overstatement, philosopher Alfred North Whitehead famously wrote, "The safest general characterization of the European philosophical tradition is that it consists of a series of footnotes to Plato."[7] When Modernity emerged in the post-Reformation world, the objectivism of the Platonists won out over Sophistic subjectivism. Moderns were interested in unchanging truth. However, when Modernity was brought to its inevitable conclusions, it retained aspects of both Sophist and Platonic thought. The centrality of a person for moral judgment (as the Sophists displayed in their actions) and for thought (as the Platonists demonstrated in their reasoning) was united in radical **immanence**—or closeness, nearness.[8] In Modernity humans with their minds and their senses solidified themselves as the measure of all truth and value, they attained autonomy—or so they thought.

B. Modernity – Autonomy in Search of Objectivity

Modernity is a set of ideas that dominated the Western world from the period shortly after the Reformation into the 20th century. It is a movement of thought that emerged out of the Enlightenment. The Enlightenment, in Philosophy, was characterized by intense wrestling with philosophical problems of knowledge.

During this time, the scientific revolution blossomed, and philosophers began to consider the relationship between the sciences—the study of that which we could sense—and ideas. On one end of the spectrum was the

---

[7] In *Process and Reality*, (Simon and Schuster, 2010), 39.

[8] **Immanence** is another key word in philosophy and theology. Like transcendence it is also a spatial term: it refers to something that is near at hand, close by. God's immanence is His presence with man. The radical immanence of modernity refers to the belief that all truth and standards of truth lay in human beings—not a distant idea or a supreme God.

empiricist David Hume.⁹ An empiricist is someone who claims that all human knowledge comes through the five senses—what we taste, touch, see, smell, and hear. David Hume (1711-1776 AD), a brilliant Scottish philosopher, was the most radical of these thinkers. For him, the human being was the centre of all knowledge. If something could not be sensed by an individual or argued from sense experience, it was not knowable. God may exist, or he may not. We have no experience of anything like "God," so his existence is a question we cannot answer. We cannot know either way. The best we can say is that maybe (just maybe) there is an explanation of the world that looks more or less (probably less) like a personal cause, to which we could give the name "God"—yet another explanation is equally likely, or better. For Hume, human experience was the final arbiter of what could be reasonably believed to be true or not.¹⁰

At the opposite end of the spectrum was a French Christian thinker named Rene Descartes (1596-1650 AD), who espoused a radical form of individualism. What is true is whatever humans can think of, beginning only with the assumption that they themselves exist.¹¹ Descartes attempted to establish all truth through deductive reasoning, through logic (e.g. If I have a generally true statement, that *lights comes from a source*; and a particular true statement, that *there is light in this room*; another statement is then true, *there is a source for the light in this room*). Descartes is famous among philosophers and theologians for the foundation of his philosophy, the claim "I think therefore I am." Descartes found certainty in the immediate, undeniable impression of self-existence. The one thing we can be sure of is our own existence, he argued, so this is the solid point from which we can reason to other truths. He then attempted to prove from this starting point of self-existence the existence of God and, from there, everything else. For Descartes, the individual and his knowledge of himself is the foundation for all other knowledge. It is true that he went on to try and prove the existence of God, yet this proof ultimately fails: all that was certain was the self.

When Modernity emerged, it was characterized by the radical

---

⁹ For empiricist, see **empiricism** in the glossary.

¹⁰ This doesn't mean "God" does not exist, only that there is no rational reason to believe that he exists, or that he has ever spoken and testified to his existence. So why believe in his existence anyway, Hume argued.

¹¹ This attempt to build all human knowledge on the foundation of a basic (or several basic) "axiom(s)" or self-evident truth(s) is called **Foundationalism**.

individualism of Descartes. The individual was the reference point for all knowledge. Truth was limited to what humans could grasp and defined based on their reason. However, objectivity was rooted in the objective world of the senses. Whatever one may say or not say about the world of ideas, the world of the senses was objectively available to the human mind and could be mastered, grasped, and manipulated.

In theology, this was manifest in the movement known as Liberal Protestantism, the attempt to make Christianity presentable and acceptable within Modernity. This project began with the assumption that something was wrong, that Christianity was not acceptable to Modern people and that this needed to be remedied. That is, it started from the perspective of humanity: we know certain truths about the world, and the Bible does not fit that mould, therefore it must be wrong—at least to some extent. The various answers that were produced all accepted the general contours of Modernity. They were all attempts to reimagine Christianity within this **worldview**, within this framework of interpretation.[12]

From Hume, these thinkers inherited the view of naturalism—the belief the world is a closed, autonomous system that is never interfered with. Humans have complete control over the phenomenal world, the world of our experience. We are free to imagine and understand it as we are able. This worldview had massive ramifications for Christian theology. Within this naturalistic, closed world, the options were endless. Jesus may have just been a moral man, proclaiming the closeness of God to the souls of every human and a radical morality centred only on love, as Adolf Harnack taught.[13]

Outside of Christianity, what emerged was the radical view we could call "scientism," the belief that scientific method—formulating hypotheses and testing them by empirical (sense-based) and repeatable tests—produced truth which could be used and trusted. The scientific method was the one and only way to objective truth. This took many different forms, but these different forms of scientism shared the belief that humans could step beyond their

---

[12] Worldview is a key concept that we will look at in the next chapter, for now it will suffice to define it as a comprehensive framework for interpreting and making decisions: it is the sum-total of ones most basic beliefs, or presuppositions, about the nature of the world, knowledge, ethics, life's purpose, etc.

[13] It is interesting how similar ideas have reappeared in the recent work of the Canadian psychologist Jordan Peterson. See my review of his book *12 Rules for Life*, https://teleioteti.ca/2018/10/11/review-of-12-rules-for-life/.

presuppositions[14] to analyse the world objectively and arrive at truth on which any likewise objective observer would agree. It is obvious why religion would be such a danger: the Bible and other holy books prevented objective analysis. They ruled out certain conclusions and demanded others before testing even began.

In its time, Modernity seemed unstoppable. By exchanging the truth of God for autonomous (i.e. independent) human study of the world, significant progress was made. Modernity seemed to find objectivity not in transcendence, in gods or ideas, but in immanence, the human analysis of objective reality. Without a universal, transcendent standard of truth, Modernity sought a firm foundation for knowledge in the objective study of the world. Unfortunately, by placing such weight on the human interpreter, Modernity shot itself in the foot. As it turns out, we humans are not nearly as objective or morally unbiased as we thought!

C. Postmodernity – Autonomy Arriving at Radical Relativity

While Modernity was producing results, great technological advancement was being made; it became more and more apparent that scientists and philosophers still disagreed. If they were analysing objectively the same reality, why would they come up with differing conclusion? How could entire generations be wrong? In the philosophy of science, the idea of a paradigm and paradigm shift was formulated. It was shown that scientists did not analyse nature objectively but according to previous theories. They did so and even dismissed contrary evidence until enough evidence emerged and enough of a consensus was attained to topple the previous interpretive paradigm. In other words, philosophers at this time began to consider the beliefs that people used to interpret the world around them: they argued that people do not see the world objectively but through an interpretive lens. Instead of looking at the world with undistorted vision, it was argued that we look through coloured glasses.

These glasses may obscure some details while giving incredible focus to others; they might readily reveal some truths but conceal and dismiss others.

---

[14] A presupposition is one of our foundational beliefs by which we automatically—without deliberate thought—interpret all our experience and form which we do all our reasoning.

These glasses were worldviews, the different interpretive frameworks every individual uses to interpret their experience. A worldview consists of all the most basic beliefs an individual has about what exists, what is truth, how truth is attained, what is right and wrong, etc. All humans have a worldview. The supposed objectivity of science was really the dominance of a single worldview. This worldview could be, and has been from time to time, overthrown (such a revolution was called a *paradigm shift*). Despite this shift in the understanding of science, from pure objectivity to the paradigm, science has continued strong. Yet other areas of thought have not been so lucky.

With the possibility of transcendence (of something beyond a person governing truth, whether a personal god or an idea) being abandoned and then the objectivity of the individual lost, the results for morality and philosophy were inevitable. If nothing greater than I tells me what is right or wrong, and my interpretation of the world around me is different from everyone else's, then the only standard for morality remaining is myself. Therefore, each individual is the standard of right and wrong, truth and falsehood. It is ultimately up to the individual to determine what is right or wrong. In the philosophy of continental Europe, this escalated quickly. Even the possibility of communication has been questioned. It is from these philosophical roots that our present situation has emerged.

This is where we find ourselves now. Morality is determined by preference and feeling, imposed on others by majority opinion. Truth is discarded in favour of one-sided tolerance—tolerance of anything that buys into the relativistic agenda. This tolerance rejects anything that suggests it is right and something else is wrong. In our schools, reading is less about understanding what a text is saying and more about analysing our response as readers to it. In Postmodernity, the autonomous search for knowledge that characterizes the history of philosophy found its end. Instead of finding a firm foundation for thought, Postmodernity found that autonomous human thinking could only result in radical relativity.

Throughout our history, humans have exchanged the truth of God for a lie, worshipping and serving the creature rather than the Creator. By pursuing this lie, we have dug ourselves an ever-deepening hole without a ladder for escape. Yet we are not without hope.

If rejecting God was what got us here in the first place, turning back to him and his revelation is undoubtedly the answer to our crisis. In our attempt to return to God, it seems wisest to begin with the questions we have just seen, namely our interaction with the world outside of us and the possibility of knowing it. That is, we will start with the questions of subjectivity and objectivity. Looking here at the fundamental problems that have shaped our contemporary crisis, we will see more clearly why rejecting God has resulted in such chaos. Concerning subjectivity, we must ask if we can interpret the world we experience without any assumptions (or presuppositions) prejudicing our results. Concerning objectivity, we must ask if objectivity is necessary for truth.

Further Reading[15]

J. P. Moreland, *Scientism & Secularism* [I-A]
John Frame, *Apologetics: A Justification of Christian Belief* [B]
* John Frame, *The Doctrine of the Knowledge of God* [I]
* John Frame, *A History of Western Philosophy and Theology* [B-I]
Ronald Nash, *Worldviews in Conflict* [B]
C.S. Lewis, *Miracles* [B]
Francis Schaeffer, *The God Who Is There* [B]

---

[15] The following resources range from (relatively) easy to quite difficult in their readability. I mark the easier reads with a **B**, those a bit more difficult with an **I**, and the most difficult with **A**. I adduce difficulty on the basis of the depth of content, knowledge presupposed by the author, and the clarity of the writing. An asterisk before a book indicates that it is especially recommended.

—PART 1—
OUR EPISTEMOLOGICAL SITUATION

WORLDVIEW THINKING: APPROPRIATE SUBJECTIVITY

> For the word of the cross is folly to those who are perishing, but to us who are being saved it is the power of God. – 1 Corinthians 1:18

Why is it that some hear of Jesus's death on the cross and resurrection and reject the historicity of these events or their significance? Why do some people stubbornly maintain that resurrections are impossible or interpret Jesus's life and death as a mere tragedy that befell one of the world's greatest moral teachers? Why is it that some scoff at the thought of God becoming a man and dying for his people while others revel in the glorious truth contained therein—that they are free, free from sin, free from wrath, free to enjoy God forever! A great part of it is surely rebellion, stubborn-hearted resistance to God (e.g. Rom 8:5-8). Yet this sinful rebellion manifests in interpretive blindness, a continual misinterpretation. "How is it," we may ask, "that someone can refuse any evidence presented and maintain that resurrections cannot happen?" But if someone comes to the table already believing this to be impossible, if they evaluate the claim that a dead man is no longer dead through this lens—that God does not exist and that miracles do not happen—they will of course reject it. As far as they are concerned, it is impossible! The problem is not whether miracles can or cannot happen, but whether it is possible that they could happen in the world that someone believes to exist. Their **worldview** is governing their interpretation; their "rose-coloured glasses," as Cornelius Van Til used to say, blind them to the possibility that God could raise someone from the dead.

They are wearing glasses, but we are too. Approaching the claims of a miracle from a position of faith in Yahweh, the God of the Bible, it is obvious that he who created the world by the word of his power and called into existence all that exists from nothing could resurrect a dead man. Furthermore, nothing but the sheer incredulity of it prevents him from entering his creation! The truth is that we are all wearing coloured glasses through which we interpret the world. But, as we will see in the next chapter, this does not make truth unattainable.

If we are wearing glasses, we need to understand how they affect our experience and interpretation. We also need to know how different worldviews affect the way others think. This is the purpose of this chapter. I want us to see what a worldview is, why they matter, and—more importantly—how a Biblical worldview helps us to navigate the troubled waters of Western culture.

I have already described a worldview as a comprehensive framework for interpreting the world; this definition focuses on the practical implications of a worldview. A worldview is often considered to be the sum of a person or society's convictions about the world. There is truth to this definition, in the sense that a worldview involves all a person's beliefs as they shape their perception and interpretation of the world. However, these "beliefs" are often implicit—rarely acknowledged or observed. Moreover, in addition to "beliefs," the worldview or "tacit framework" (to use Polanyi's term) involves many non-propositional forms of knowledge. That is, our worldview involves conceptual knowledge and person-knowledge which cannot be captured by a statement such as "I believe that …." We will discuss this unseen depth of worldview in *The Gift of Seeing*. For now, we will focus on the tip of the iceberg, those conscious and unconscious beliefs that can be expressed with some ease in a statement such as, "I believe that …." This aspect of a worldview is sometimes called a philosophy or a theology, a systematic interpretation of the world.[1] Our worldviews involve our beliefs

---

[1] From a Christian perspective, the difference between "theology" and "philosophy" is not so much that one is religious and the other a-religious. The difference is that theology deals with the world from revelation and philosophy from reason. Because reason is ultimately a gift from God, an interpretive tool for interpreting his revelation in Scripture and the world, and is itself a part of natural revelation, philosophy for a Christian is properly a subset of theology—the Word of God applied to the realm of reason and logic.

about the existence or non-existence of God and what he is like, about the relationship between humanity and God, one human to another, humanity to animals, etc.[2] All our fundamental beliefs, our assumptions that lie behind all our thinking, make up our worldview. The possibility of miracles is a key belief of the Biblical worldview, an implication of the belief that God is the Lord of his creation and active (or immanent) within it.

Philosophers have generally summarized a worldview as that which we believe about what exists (metaphysics), how we know (epistemology), and what is right and wrong (ethics). This book is an effort to unpack one aspect of the Biblical worldview, its epistemology. Epistemology ultimately concerns the "how" question or method of thinking, how to engage in intellectual thought—if we can at all.

In this chapter, we will look at what worldviews *do* more than any specific worldview. We have already considered various features of the Modern and Postmodern worldview in the last chapter and will continue to do so where necessary, but our focus will not be so much on what Postmoderns believe but why it matters that they believe these things.

A worldview is all of a person's beliefs that form a comprehensive framework with which they interpret the world. "Seeing is not believing," writes C.S. Lewis, "For this reason, the question whether miracles occur can never be answered simply by experience."[3] Seeing is not believing because sight must be interpreted: if someone sees a miracle and believes with the utmost conviction that miracles are impossible, they will insist that it was an illusion—for miracles just don't happen! Our worldview factors into every decision we make, and we should be grateful that it does! When we prepare to cross a busy road, we do not have to think about whether it is wise or not to jump in front of a car: we know that to do so is foolish and deadly. But why do we know this? We know this because we believe in causality (that causes produce effects) and that the effect of being hit by a car is serious

---

[2] James N. Anderson helpfully summarizes the major beliefs of a worldview as TAKES, as in "what it TAKES to make a worldview." *Theology*, what is the absolute in your worldview? *Anthropology*, what do you believe about man? *Knowledge*, what is truth and how do we get it? *Ethics*, what is right or wrong, good or bad? And *Salvation*, what is the problem with the world and how is it fixed?

[3] C. S Lewis, *Miracles: A Preliminary Study* (New York: Harper Collins, 2011), chap. 1.

injury or death. This is a belief based on experience and the testimony of others (maybe a parent reprimanding us as a child) that we use to make basic decisions every day. For Christians, the belief that God exists and cares for his children leads us to pray in difficult circumstances. The belief that he is the source of all good gifts leads us to give thanks at meals and before bed.

The list would be endless if we attempted to analyse all the beliefs that shape our everyday actions, and we would miss many so-called "tacit" beliefs—those that we are not regularly aware of. Worldviews shape all that we do, so it matters that we get them right! What would happen if we did not believe that effects follow from causes? Would we be so hesitant about jumping in front of cars? Surely we would not live long without that belief!

If we do not believe that truth is attainable, we will not accept the truth claims of the Bible. If we do not believe that miracles happen, we will not believe the resurrection. Getting our worldview right is of vital importance, our lives in this age and the age to come rest on what we believe and do not believe. We must, then, know how we can be sure of the Christian worldview, we must refine our own worldview, and we must know how to interact with others. The remaining pages of this chapter will begin addressing these needs, looking at how worldviews are formed and how this affects the way we evaluate them. In the next chapter, we will consider how we can be sure of the Christian worldview, how we can reason with those with whom we disagree, and how we can refine our worldviews.

We have considered beliefs as the content of a worldview, but we have yet to look at how we can evaluate our own worldview and the worldviews of others. To learn this, we need to consider the beginning of a worldview, how we come to adopt the worldview we have. Someone may argue that they have done so by reason, claiming that this was the worldview that seemed most reasonable to them. Yet this is not the real explanation. Our worldviews originate a little earlier. Worldviews begin with a recipe of three ingredients, all of which rely on faith, not reason.

Our worldview begins with what we could call **innate ideas**, that is, ideas that we do not and cannot learn from experience, for experience requires them.[4] For example, we are born with knowledge of **the law of non-**

---

[4] We will consider innate ideas a little more in Chapter 10.

contradiction, the principle that no object or idea can be itself and its opposite at the same time in the same way. The letter A cannot be whatever is not-A at the same time, nor can $2 + 3 = 5$ and 6 at the same time and in the same way. A computer cannot be fully black and fully white in the same way and at the same time, though it could have a fully black layer on top of a fully white one. A phone cannot be totally unbroken and totally broken simultaneously. Such examples could be multiplied endlessly. Without this law, learning is impossible. For example, though I burned my hand on the stove once, it is possible that I could not burn it in the exact same circumstances. Furthermore, without the law of non-contradiction, all thought is nonsense: I could be black and white, male and female, up and down, left and right, bee or bird, human or monkey, in space or on earth, this or that, at any time and in any way.[5] Barring disability, we are also born with the concepts necessary to interpret light as different colours and to interpret this light in order to produce a mental picture. As children, we do not wait to prove innate ideas before we use them; we trust that they are correct and employ them intuitively. Innate ideas are not enough, however, for they are only tools necessary to interpret *experience*.

We also learn our worldview from experience, especially from others telling us what to believe (e.g. that the sound "food" can be used to describe and request an edible substance required to live). For example, we learn about Jesus Christ and his saving work by hearing the word of the Gospel preached (Rom 10:14-18). According to Romans 1:18-32, we learn from experiencing every part of creation—ourselves surely included—that Yahweh exists, what his character is like, and that we should honour and thank him. This brings us to the third ingredient of our worldview: it is composed of one part innate ideas, one part experience, and one part rebellion.

That is, we all reject what we learn about God from experience and innate ideas. We reject his Lordship, his demands upon us, and replace the Creator with the creature, with ourselves—even as babies (Ps 51:5)! It is important to observe that these are not baking instructions (add innate ideas, followed by experience, then season with rebellion) but an ingredient list: all of these co-exist as we develop; none is first. With trust—apart from careful reason—we

---

[5] If the statements "J. Alexander Rutherford is floating in space, not on earth, at 10:30 am, Nov. 11, 2017" and "J. Alexander Rutherford is on earth, not in space, at 10:30 am, Nov. 11, 2017" are both true, than any contradictory state can be true (e.g. it is only snowing and only not-snowing at the same time in the same place).

accept the testimony of our minds, of our senses and others, and we trust ourselves over God. The natural worldview of humans is part truth and part lie, postured in rebellion towards God (cf. Rom 8:6-7). As we mature, we learn different things from different sources and arrive at a fuller and fuller interpretation of the world around us, eventually arriving at our present state.

You may be asking yourself at this time why you need an ingredient list. The point of looking at these ingredients is to notice that nobody forms a worldview like Descartes: none of us are born an empty hard drive to be filled by logical deduction (I exist, my existence requires God, God's existence means others exist, etc.) or experience (I experience my own existence, the existence of others, the existence of trees, of goodness, of badness, etc.). So if someone expects us to prove our worldview from one of these routes, they will be sorely disappointed! There is no objective state by which any human can step back and neutrally evaluate their own or another's worldview. All such evaluation comes from within a worldview.

A Christian needs to begin evaluating his own worldview on its terms; a Hindu must evaluate his worldview on its terms; an atheist on his; etc. This may lead us to think that we are stuck at an impasse—you have your worldview and I have mine! But this is not the conclusion we need to or should draw. This is the conclusion our culture arrives at, namely, that a lack of objectivity means there is no truth. I began this book, however, claiming that this was not the case, that the Bible provides us with a way beyond this impasse. I am not ready to give up and neither should you be. In the next chapter, we will see how we can still reason and arrive at truth despite the subjectivity our worldviews give us.

Another Perspective on Subjectivity

In this chapter, we have seen that knowing involves a subjective aspect; we all approach the world with an interpretive lens. However, another question arises when begin to think this way. Why is it that two people with the same worldview come to different interpretations of the same object or event? Consider the four Gospels: each comes from the perspective of someone who was with or learned from those who were with Jesus, yet each is distinctively different. Consider another example:

why can the act of a man walking through a doorway be alternatively interpreted as, "the man came home"; "the man went inside"; "the man walked through the door;" "the man entered the building"; or "daddy's home!!!"? All of these describe the same event from different perspectives, different ways of viewing it from different spatial viewpoints (came into the home, went inside) or understandings of its significance ("daddy's home!" and "the man entered the home" are very different in this sense).

Yet, all of these are true. God knows all possible perspectives, and so these all are part of God's multi-faceted interpretation of his universe. Each of us only has a partial perspective, for we face several limitations (e.g. I can only see something from one perspective at a time). Therefore, we possess truth but not all truth. There is, therefore, great benefit to be gained from learning with other people who share our worldview, from not limiting ourselves to only our perspective. Returning to the four Gospels, each gives us a true perspective that enriches our understanding of Jesus Christ and his work: we would be impoverished if we lost one! We can also learn from those who disagree at a worldview level, for there is truth to be found even in a rebellious worldview, something we will see further in the next chapter.

Further Reading

John Frame, *the Doctrine of the Knowledge of God* [I]
* John Frame, *Apologetics: a Justification of Christian Belief* [B]
John Frame, *Systematic Theology*, pgs. 36-50 [B-I]
John Frame, *A History of Western Philosophy and Theology*, pgs. 1-41 [B-I]
Ronald Nash, *Worldviews in Conflict* [B]
C.S. Lewis, *Miracles* [B]
Francis Schaeffer, *The God Who Is There* [B]
Vern Poythress, *Symphonic Theology* [I-A]

3

THE TRUTH IS OUT THERE: APPROPRIATE OBJECTIVITY

> Sanctify them in the truth; your word is truth. – John 17:17

We left the last chapter on a cliff hanger: how can we reason with someone from another **worldview**? Can we be sure ours is true? Yet, common sense already answers this question: some worldviews simply must be wrong! Surely it cannot be as equally true that jumping in front of a car will not kill me as is my certainty that it will. It cannot be as equally true—or even as likely to be true—to claim that I am the only being in existence as to claim that my senses are trustworthy and others exist.

We are not left with common sense alone, however, for Scripture tells us clearly that truth is out there, and his name is Yahweh. According to Jesus, he is "the way, *the Truth*, and the life" (John 14:6, emphasis added) and his word is truth (John 17:17). God is true, and in him is no lie (Num 23:19, Rom 3:1-8). God cannot deceive—he does not lie—nor can he be wrong: he is Truth, and he knows all things (Job 38-41; Isa 40:28, 46:10). If God is true, if truth is his thoughts, his interpretation of his creation and himself, then truth is whatever corresponds—however partially[1]—to his thoughts. If God's thoughts are what is true, and any truth we have is an interpretation of the world and God that corresponds to his thoughts, we can define truth in

---

[1] This an important clarification: our thoughts never fully correspond to God's. His thoughts are different both in quality (He knows all things because He created them; we know what we know because we experience them) and extent (we know some things partially; He knows all things wholly).

this way: *Truth is an appropriate interpretation of reality, one that corresponds—partially yet without error—to God's interpretation.*[2] An interpretation is true not if it is complete but if it contains no error—nothing contrary to God's interpretation. Knowing what truth is and that humans can apprehend it, we need to ask, how do we go about gaining it? How do we acquire truth and be sure that it corresponds to God's thoughts?

We arrive at a right interpretation, and so truth, by perceiving the creation and God's revelation in Scripture through the senses he has given us and interpreting it through the lens of his revelation.[3] We know that our interpretations correspond to his by interacting with his world, trusting in the senses he has given us; by thinking about his world, trusting the minds he has given us; and doing all this in submission to his verbal revelation.

If truth is available to human beings, we are then left with the problem of other worldviews, how we explain their existence. The answer from Scripture is that human beings "by their unrighteousness suppress the truth" (Rom. 1:18). If all humans reject the truth as God has revealed it, the question we should ask is not why other worldviews exist but why there is any truth at all in other worldviews. There is truth in other worldviews because this unrighteous suppression of truth is not complete: God is gracious and does not allow human sin to abound to the extent that it possibly could.

This gracious act of restraint is often called common grace: this aspect of common grace is not explicitly taught in Scripture, but Romans 2 (especially verse 14) and Acts 17:28 indicate that despite their sinful suppression of truth, someone who is not a Christian maintains some truth in their worldview. This is verified by our own experience (which Scripture also affirms, see ch. 10).

We see, then, that truth exists, and it is found through God's revelation

---

[2] Defining truth in this way implicitly rejects the typical ontology of the Western tradition. Traditionally, Western philosophy has held to various forms of metaphysical realism, the belief that ideas or truths have a real existence. By identify truth as an interpretation of reality, I have inextricably linked truth to the interpreting subject, to the mind that interpret. For more on this, see Chapter 10 of this volume and Volume 3, *The Gift of Seeing* on **abstraction**.

[3] God has revealed himself in the created order, but truth implies an interpretation: "a rock" is not a truth, but "there are rocks" is. Therefore, it seems that God's revelation in nature must have two parts: the creation of *right functioning faculties* to interpret the *clear evidence of Himself within the created world*.

in Scripture and through interpreting his creation. We see also that worldviews abound and that each worldview has its own test of truth—an atheist will surely not concede that God's interpretation is the measure of truth! Therefore, we need a way to reason with someone who disagrees with us on such a fundamental level. We may do so in three ways: by showing them that our own worldview is true; by showing that their own worldview is false *according to its own criteria of truth*; and by appealing to the knowledge of the truth they have rebelliously suppressed.[4] Considering these three ways by which those of differing worldviews can interact serves our purpose by revealing a way beyond the impasse of relativism, showing us that worldviews may be right or wrong and that this can be shown.

Furthermore, understanding how to rationally defend or criticize a worldview helps us to be firm in our faith, to understand the differences we see in the views around us, and to navigate difficult **apologetic** discussions—intellectually presenting the Christian faith.[5] That being said, let us consider three ways we can interact with other worldviews.

A. Showing a Worldview to Be True

A worldview can only be proven false if it self-destructs or true if it is self-verifying. Defensively, we then need to show that our worldview is self-verifying, not self-destructing. Three tests help us here. All worldviews function to interpret their authority and the world, and so guide our actions. A worldview must therefore 1) be self-consistent on its own terms, 2) it must appropriately correspond to reality as interpreted on its own terms, and 3) it must be functional on its own terms.

First, a worldview must be self-consistent. A self-consistent worldview is not one in which there are no tensions but in which tensions are explained by that worldview. The Bible contains tensions, yet it tells us to expect them

---

[4] These three categories are roughly parallel to John Frame's three approaches to apologetic discussion: defence, offense, and proof. Cf. *Apologetics: A Justification of Christian Belief.*

[5] By apologetics, we do not imply being apologetic—sorry for our beliefs. Apologetics comes from a Greek word meaning to make a defense (cf. 1 Peter 3:15). Apologetics is sometimes defined as the rational defence of the Christian faith.

because God has all truth and has not shared it with us (e.g. Deut 29:29). If a worldview says at one point "this is true" and at another point, "this is not true," without an explanation of what has changed, this is self-destructive. For example, the Koran says that the *Injeel*, the books about Jesus, is God's word;[6] yet elsewhere it denies the crucifixion and resurrection of Jesus Christ, which the New Testament, particularly the Gospels or *Injeel*, affirms. Of course, the Muslim will claim that the New Testament has been corrupted—that it is not the true *Injeel*—yet they have no reason from history or the Koran to claim this. This is an internal contradiction. In contrast, the Bible commands food laws in one part and repudiates them in another, but it explains that this is not a contradiction. Instead, it is a change in **covenant**.

Second, a worldview must correspond to reality as it interprets it. The Bible teaches that it is God's Word and thus absolutely authoritative. Its own testimony is our primary reason for believing it to be so, but we can support its claim by showing that it claims this consistently. Subjectively, we can support the Bible's internal claim by an appeal to the Holy Spirit's attestation: the Bible claims that God's people will hear his voice, recognize him speaking in Scripture (cf. John 10:27, 2 Cor 4:1-6). I testify that I experience this when I read it. Yet this will not persuade someone who does not yet recognize God's voice. Because a worldview must correspond to reality as it interprets it, we can show how the claims the Bible makes about reality—objective morality, truth, a beginning of creation, certain historical facts, etc.—correspond to reality as we experience it. An atheist will of course object to our interpretation of reality, but we can argue that if you assume the Biblical worldview, all our experience is completely consistent with it. If a worldview says something about reality that its other claims about reality contradict, this is also a form of self-destruction. If a worldview says, "trust your senses" and then denies the existence of other people, it has denied the first claim with the second.

Third, a worldview must be liveable on its own terms: if it says you are to deny causality and so step in front of moving cars but simultaneously calls you to preserve your own life at all costs, this is a self-destruction in liveableness. That is, to follow both precepts consistently would end your life and contradict both.

---

[6] To be exact, the Muslim's claim that the *Injeel* was a book given *by* Jesus, yet it is clear that what is being referred to is what we today call the Gospels or maybe the entire New Testament, the books *about* Jesus. E.g. Sura 5:46, 47a; Sura 57:27.

As a Christian, then, we show that the Bible claims its own authority and we give examples of how it does so consistently, answering objections with Biblical answers. We also show how it gives a consistent interpretation of our world and that it is liveable (on its own terms). Doing this gives us great confidence in the Bible, in conjunction with its self-attestation, yet is rarely persuasive.

The strongest internal claim the Bible makes is that it is the only accurate, or true, interpretation of reality. That is, the Bible claims that every other worldview is wrong and therefore will fail at some point. We can thus sketch what the Biblical worldview is, answer some objections, and then focus on the next two forms of worldview evaluation. Going on the offensive, we show how all other worldviews self-destruct and we appeal to the knowledge of God that all people have. In the latter case, we make arguments from creation that presuppose the Biblical worldview but find resonance in the inconsistent remnants of this worldview others have.

B. Showing a Worldview to be Self-Destructing

If everyone has exchanged the truth for a lie, and the Bible is true, every other view must be (somewhat of) a lie. The question is, how is it a lie—how does it self-destruct? Finding the lie takes great patience and discernment. We need to listen to another person, truly understand what they believe, and see how their rejection of a Biblical truth leads them into contradiction. Now, showing someone a contradiction in their worldview takes great wisdom and gentleness, so identification is only half the battle. Consider, though, an example from a Postmodern worldview. Many who would accept the relativity of moral and religious belief hold to science and reason as valid ways of knowing, valid tools for understanding reality. However, neither reason nor empirical science is sufficient to affirm the existence of anything outside oneself—or even a definition of the "self."

Let me explain. The Bible tells us that God made the world around us and gave us trustworthy senses. The Bible teaches the existence of more than just me; it teaches the existence of God and fellow human beings. This all makes sense, and it would be ridiculous to deny it! Because the primary authority of our worldview tells us others exist and our senses, which are trustworthy, tell us others exist, we have good reason to believe this. However, if we assume a worldview where the individual and his or her mind is the final authority, the measure of truth, then it is *unreasonable* to believe in the existence of others.

Beginning with reason, as Descartes did, can you prove anything outside of your mind? What principle of reason would allow you to prove that I exist: could I not just be a figment of your imagination and this book the product of a dream? Beginning with **empiricism**, what reason do we have for believing that our senses correspond to reality? What test can we run that does not assume the existence of trustworthy senses? Assuming the authority of the self, nothing in our mind or experience justifies us in trusting our senses. If we cannot trust our senses, we have no reason to believe anything exists but the self—which we know exists only because the very act of denying our own existence proves it (remember Descartes, "I think therefore I am"). Yet, even the sort of "existence" we have is up for grabs.

Any definition of self that moves beyond "I think" relies on the senses. Do I have a body or not? How would I know if I did from my mind or unreliable senses? How, based on a worldview where the self is the ultimate authority, would someone prove that he or she is not a computer program, a brain in a jar, or even a bumblebee? If someone told us we were a human being in a physical world populated by human beings, how could we know he or she was not a figment of our imagination or a program with the very purpose of assuaging our doubts? If the self is the ultimate authority, this is where we find ourselves—yet Christians need not fear this end.

God has not left us without a testimony. He has spoken and affirmed our senses, our minds, and the existence of others. Praise our Lord that he has not left us without a witness, that he has not left us to our autonomous selves, adrift on an open sea, floating as if through an infinite nothing!

Postmodern worldviews are equally self-destructing in the area of morality. Most Postmoderns would not subscribe to purely relativistic morality—something is right because you desire it—but tend to pick and choose what aspects of morality they want to adhere to. In Canada, one's physical sex is not considered significant in identifying one's gender, and Christian sexual ethics are dismissed. Yet, those who lobby for legislation protecting the LGBTQ+ community are the same community who respond (rightfully!) with outrage to the many sexual assaults and rapes reported on university campuses. In one case, they reject one standard of morality—the

Christian understanding of sexuality—and lobby for legislation that requires radical sexual tolerance. In another case, they defend a different aspect of Christian morality. What reason does their worldview give for rejecting Christian sexuality while enforcing sexual ethics regarding rape? By what standard do they do so? Their worldview provides no such standard.

This has long been recognized as the problem with naturalism, the belief that only nature exists: it gives no reason for morality, no standard by which to measure one action as wrong and another as right. These two examples reveal some ways that postmodern worldviews—the most prevalent worldviews in Western society—self-destruct. Yet these are not the only tools in our tool belt. If someone was completely consistent and reasonable, then showing such flaws would always be effective, yet this is not always the case. The reason for this is that no non-Christian worldview is completely consistent. No one is completely successful in suppressing the truth of God. This is why some truth can be found in these worldviews.

C. Appealing to the Truth Suppressed in Unrighteousness

A 20th century Christian theologian named Cornelius Van Til would illustrate this worldview-borrowing by picturing a child being held up by her father and slapping him in the face: it is only because the father holds the child up that she is able to attack him. The only reason a non-Christian worldview can disagree with and assail the Christian worldview is because they are resting on its foundation: they are living off borrowed capital. If the Christian worldview is the truth that has been exchanged for a lie, and this exchange is only partial, then what remains of the truth is a remnant of the Christian worldview. This means that there is common ground between a Christian and a Non-Christian. This common ground is not found in some neutral, objective fact on which both can agree. In fact, there are none: all facts are interpreted by a worldview. Any common ground is found in the vestiges of Christian truth, in the knowledge of God, that lays suppressed and buried within other worldviews. By drawing on this common ground, showing how all creation points to the Creator, we can—as the Holy Spirit works on their heart—bring this truth uncomfortably to the surface. This is where traditional apologetic arguments can be quite helpful.

The 18th century empiricist David Hume conclusively showed that on non-Christian assumptions—that the self was the ultimate authority—

traditional Christian apologetic arguments failed.[7] For example, we often argue that creation has an element of design in it. This makes sense when we assume as part of our worldview a designer, yet Hume pointed out that "designer" in this argument is not God but a mere human, for this is the only cause we know to produce such effects. If the design argument proves any designer, argued Hume, the designer is a finite being like humans. Furthermore, we could observe that "design" means something completely different for a non-Christian than for a Christian. For the former, it is an amazingly improbably coincidence, yet perfectly possible—for God is already ruled out as an explanation. His foot cannot be allowed to slip through the door![8] In contrast, for the Christian, design is evidence for the designer. Two different worldviews furnish the same empirical observations with different interpretations. Yet, the design argument makes intuitive sense and has convinced some people of the truth of Christianity. From what we have seen, it is evident why it sometimes succeeds. If even the most ardent atheist is suppressing the knowledge of the truth of God, then evidence of a designer corresponds to that suppressed belief. If the Holy Spirit graciously grants a repentant heart, such an argument exposes the truth being denied and reveals our rebellion.

The same can be said for the cosmological argument, which has come to the forefront in Christian apologetics through the work of William Lane Craig. Craig and others argue in this way:

---

[7] David Hume, *Dialogues Concerning Natural Religion*, Dover Philosophical Classics (Mineola, N.Y.: Dover Publications, 2006).

[8] The Atheist Richard C. Lewontin once made this startling admission in a review for *The New York Review of Books*, "Our willingness to accept scientific claims that are against common sense is the key to an understanding of the real struggle between science and the supernatural. We take the side of science *in spite* of the patent absurdity of some of its constructs, *in spite* of its failure to fulfill many of its extravagant promises of health and life, *in spite* of the tolerance of the scientific community for unsubstantiated just-so stories, because we have a prior commitment, a commitment to materialism. It is not that the methods and institutions of science somehow compel us to accept a material explanation of the phenomenal world, but, on the contrary, that we are forced by our *a priori* adherence to material causes to create an apparatus of investigation and a set of concepts that produce material explanations, no matter how counter-intuitive, no matter how mystifying to the uninitiated. Moreover, that materialism is absolute, for we cannot allow a Divine Foot in the door." (No emphasis added.)

- we know that everything that begins to exist has a cause (e.g. a car is made, a baby is conceived),
- the universe we live in began to exist,
- therefore, the universe we live in has a cause.[9]

We must then ask, what could be the cause of the world? It is then argued that only God, a being without a beginning, is the adequate cause for the world.[10] On atheistic presuppositions, Hume takes issue with this argument as well.

He wonders if the world itself could not be necessary—like the laws of mathematics—or if a chain of such causes itself needs an explanation. From experience, we know that a cause needs an explanation (if a car moves, we are right to ask why), but we have no experience of an infinite succession of causes, so experience cannot show that God is required to explain the world. Many atheists argue similarly today, suggesting that our world is one of many universes that come in and out of existence eternally.[11] Yet, as with the design

---

[9] John Frame argues that the arguments for the impossibility of an infinite universe, necessitating that the universe has a beginning, only show that the idea of a infinite series is hard to grasp, not that it is inherently impossible. If we agree with Frame, he proffers the Aquinian cosmological argument as a more persuasive alternative. Namely, even an infinite universe requires a cause: everything that exists requires an explanation for its existence, the universe exists, therefore it needs an explanation. God is not an exception to this rule because He has the property of aseity; according to His own testimony, He is the explanation of His own existence. John Frame, "'Infinite Series,'" *Frame-Poythress.Org*, last modified May 21, 2012, accessed July 28, 2021, https://frame-poythress.org/infinite-series/.

[10] Craig and others often argue from the Big Bang to show the world has a beginning. Even if we are not convinced that the Big Bang is a Biblically valid explanation of creation, we could argue from the atheist's belief in the Big Bang that the world had a beginning ("even your own belief proves my point"). Cf. William Lane Craig, *The Kalam Cosmological Argument* (Eugene, OR: Wipf and Stock Publishers, 2000); William Lane Craig, *On Guard: Defending Your Faith With Reason And Precision* (Colorado Springs, Colo.: David C. Cook, 2010).

This argument at first does not prove that the world had an uncaused cause—a Creator who is Himself not created—yet they argue that eventually you need one, so logically it is best to explain the creation of the world by God (using the philosophical principle of parsimony).

[11] We could go beyond Hume and argue that if our self is the ultimate criteria of truth, and the primary data for logic comes from senses, we have no experience of space and time coming into existence (we have only experienced the coming into existence of things existing in space and time), so "cause" in the above argument is

argument, this argument is often convincing. Though it does not make complete sense within an atheistic worldview, it does within the Christian worldview, so it may resonate with the truth that is suppressed in unrighteousness.

In this chapter we have seen that despite the subjective aspect of all knowing—even though interpretation is an inevitable and essential aspect of knowing—truth is out there; his name is Yahweh. The teaching of Scripture (what I have been calling the Christian worldview) gives us a solid foundation from which we can know truth and explains how we can interact with those who have a different worldview. We have seen three different ways that we as Christians could interact with those who have a different worldview. Yet such a discussion is most effective when all of the above are appropriately considered: when we consider how Christianity explains the world, how non-Christian views do not, and how the created world testifies to God.

In this chapter's discussion, we have seen that at the heart of the struggle between Christianity and non-Christian worldviews is the question of authority. It is here that Christianity is shown to be strongest and where its answer to the epistemological crisis of the West is found, and so it is to the question of authority that we must now turn.

Transcendental Arguments

I would be remiss if I did not mention the transcendental argument in this context. Among certain circles, the primary—sometimes the only—apologetic argument for the Christian faith is an argument which Cornelius Van Til called the transcendental argument. For our purposes, we can consider the transcendental argument as a specific way of bringing together the three methods above to interact with a non-Christian worldview.

Essentially, a transcendental argument argues for the truth of Christianity by showing that the Christian worldview is the presupposition of rational thought, so that denying the Christian worldview actually affirms it. That is, a transcendental argument for

not precise enough to make a logically sound argument. The argument "equivocates," uses two different meanings for its key word.

Christianity argues that to be able to deny Christianity you have to assume it is true, that the very possibility of denying or affirming anything presupposes that Christianity is right. It is not, therefore, an argument that tries to prove one piece or another of the Christian worldview, such as the resurrection or existence of God, but an argument that seeks to show that reality, knowledge, morality, etc. only make sense if the Christian worldview is true. In the words of Cornelius Van Til,

> the best and only possible proof for the existence of [the sovereign God of Christianity] is that his existence is required for the uniformity of nature and for the coherence of all things in the world. We cannot *prove* the existence of beams underneath a floor if by proof we mean that they must be ascertainable in the way that we can see the chairs and tables of the room. But the very idea of a floor as the support of tables and chairs requires the idea of beams that are underneath. But there would be no floor if no beams were underneath…. Even non-Christians presuppose [the truth of Christian theism] while they verbally reject it. They need to presuppose the truth of Christian theism in order to account for their own accomplishments.[i]

Traditionally, the transcendental argument has been presented in this *objective* sense: unless the Christian God exists, reason is impossible. Or, to deny the Christian God, someone must actually assume He exists. However, in this book I am developing a transcendental argument of a different sort, what we could call the *subjective transcendental argument*.

That is, the traditional transcendental argument considers what has to be the case, whether you acknowledge it or not. Even though an atheist denies God, their very denial presupposes that he exists. Therefore, your act of denying God demonstrates that he exists. It is an argument from any point in a worldview to the necessity of God's existence. I am arguing in this book that God's existence is not only objectively necessary for knowledge but subjectively necessary. That is, I am arguing that apart from faith in God and submission to him, there is no subjective ground for knowledge; the only option other than faith in God, if one were to be consistent, is complete scepticism. The only way to reasonably uphold reason is to submit to God as he has revealed himself in his word. The other option, which most non-Christian philosophers accept, is to build reason on an irrational basis. For example, many forms of foundationalism say that belief in the reliability of the senses is properly basic, it is "rational" for anyone to believe it. However, they are unable to give any rational reason for the belief that the reliability of the senses is rational. So instead of arguing for the existence of God, I am arguing for faith and submission to God.

ⁱ*The Defense of the Faith*, 2nd Edition (Presbyterian and Reformed, 1963), 103.

Further Reading

Cornelius Van Til, *Christian Theistic Evidences* [A]
Cornelius Van Til, *The Defense of the Faith* [A]
David Hume, *Dialogues Concerning Natural Religion* [A]
Francis Schaeffer, *He Is There and He is not Silent* [B]
Gregory Bahnsen, *Van Til's Apologetic: Readings and Analysis* [A][12]
John Frame, *The Doctrine of the Knowledge of God* [I]
*John Frame, *Apologetics: A Justification of Christian Belief* [B]
John Frame, "Infinite Series," https://frame-poythress.org/infinite-series/ [I]
Paul Chamberlain, *Can We Be Good Without God?* [B]
William Lane Craig, *On Guard: Defending Your Faith with Reason and Precision* [B-I]
William Lane Craig, *The Kalam Cosmological Argument* [I]

---

[12] Bahnsen's treatment is helpful and makes Van Til's thought more accessible. However, Bahnsen's development of Van Til moves in several rather unhelpful directions.

—PART 2—
THE STANDARD OF EPISTEMOLOGY

A WORD FROM BEYOND: APPROPRIATE AUTHORITY

Oh, the depth of the riches and wisdom and knowledge of God! How unsearchable are his judgments and how inscrutable his ways!

> For who has known the mind of the Lord,
>   or who has been his counselor?
> Or who has given a gift to him
>   that he might be repaid?

For from him and through him and to him are all things. To him be glory forever. Amen. – Romans 11:33-36

At the heart of a **worldview**, and the centre of the conflict between Christian and non-Christian worldviews, stands the question of final authority. When all the evidence is in, who gets the final say? What is the ruler we use to measure truth?

There are ultimately only two options available to us. According to the Bible, there are two fundamental types of existence, two groups that encompass all that exists: there are the Creator and the creature. The question of authority must rest in one of these two spheres: is the standard of truth to be found in the Creator or the created order?

By exchanging the glory and truth of God for a lie, choosing to worship the creature instead of the Creator, all non-Christian worldviews find their ultimate authority in the creature. In Modernity, the standard was thought to be objective reality—just the facts. It was thought that humans could objectively interact with the world and arrive at the same conclusions, that the universe provided objective truth to those who would observe it without bias. We saw already that this authority failed: there are no uninterpreted facts! For this reason, one authority remains, the self.

Postmodernity places final authority in the self, for it is a person who provides the interpretation of reality. This is seen most clearly in morality, as legislation is based ever more on individuals' feelings and self-perception (i.e. something is wrong if it makes me feel bad). The authority of the self is also seen in learning, where personal response and creativity are emphasized over the passing on of truth. In reading, clear communication from the writer to the reader is forsaken for the reader's response. In empirical science, authority ultimately rests on the observer's interpretation. Decisions to accept or reject a hypothesis ultimately come down to subjective proof. "Does it convince me or not" is the pressing question of the Postmodern mind. It is often not the truth that is found convincing but relativism that sets aside absolute claims (e.g. Yahweh exists) for personal convictions.

Christianity, however, identifies the final authority for morality and truth in God, not humanity or creation. The creation requires interpretation—it is not objective—but man's interpretation of it is not the measure of truth. God's interpretation is. This is, in fact, where the Christian worldview stands forth most evidently as the truth. The Bible claims that God is the standard of all truth and that all things have their existence and meaning in relation to him. He is the originator and sustainer of all the creation and all of it is created for his glory. This means that in submission to him, by believing the truth about God, we can understand him and the creation he has made.

On the other hand, this also means that apart from such a posture of submission, in rebellion against him, consistent and rational thought is impossible. Any truth we retain represents our failure to abandon God consistently. We depend on his support to rebel against him. If final authority is given to the creature, then knowledge is impossible. We are left in the same place our culture is now, with no standard of truth or morality beyond the self. To regain our footing, then, we need to regain our place in the world. We need to see ourselves as creatures in the Creator's worlds, subjects of the Creator's decrees and recipients of his gracious gifts. God has not left himself without witnesses in this world, nor has he been silent. By leaving his distinct stamp on the created order, giving people the cognitive tools necessary to read it, and by revealing himself in the Word, he has made truth readily available to all who would submit themselves before him.

In the following chapters, we will look at God as the final authority for knowing, and how creation and Scripture function to present us his authoritative interpretation of reality. Beginning with creation (chapter 4), we will then consider Scripture (chapter 5), and conclude by looking at the ethical implications that result if God is our authority for knowing (chapter 6).

Further Reading

Francis Schaeffer, *The Great Evangelical Disaster* [B]
* John Frame, *The Doctrine of the Word of God* [I]
* John Frame, *The Doctrine of the Knowledge of God* [I]

5

THE COVENANTAL REVELATION OF CREATION

> For what can be known about God is plain to them, because God has shown it to them. For his invisible attributes, namely, his eternal power and divine nature, have been clearly perceived, ever since the creation of the world, in the things that have been made. So they are without excuse. – Romans 1:19-20

From the beginning of creation, God has revealed himself to his creatures through direct spoken communication, through prophets, and through the written Scriptures. God has revealed himself in this way, yet he has not done so to everyone. But we have already seen that God has not left himself without a witness, that the very creation reveals him to everyone. This creation revelation fills two important functions according to the Bible. First, God's revelation in creation is sufficient to reveal his existence and character. Creation is an abiding testimony to his glorious power and character, giving God glory through its testimony and leading those who interpret the creation into awestruck praise (Ps 19; Acts 14:17) or rebellion. For this reason, all humans are without excuse for their rebellion against God (Rom 1:18-32). Creation also testifies to the appropriate response humans should take towards it (Rom 1:20-23, 2:14-16).

The creation does this, and it does so authoritatively: humans are held accountable for their failure to respond to God as he is revealed in the creation (Rom 1:18-32) and to act appropriately within the creation (Rom 2:12-16). It is important to recognize that these functions are covenantal: the created order guides men and women in the way appropriate to the **covenant** under which they relate to the Creator.[1]

For Adam and Eve and all their descendants, this revelation would lead them in appropriate worship and service of Yahweh. Abraham and his descendants were guided by creation revelation as interpreted in light of God's verbal revelation to fulfil the purpose he had given them. With the coming of Jesus, creation—or general—revelation guides his people in the fulfilment of the great commission, guiding us in worship, evangelism, and everyday life (e.g. it gives us common ground for evangelism, leading us to glorify God for his handiwork, and guides us in applying the Word of God to everyday life in the created order).

The purpose of this chapter is to unpack and explain three interdependent ways the creation reveals God and his ways so that these functions are fulfilled. We will consider the revelation of God in the testimony of the created world, the revelation of God in human discernment, and the revelation of God in humanity's mental faculties.

Two considerations must be kept in mind if we are to properly account for God's revelation as we experience it, namely the Fall and the resulting curse. Though the world was originally created as an efficient bearer of this revelation, it has now been corrupted by the curse. Therefore, though it is a sufficient revelation to achieve its purposes, it is often misinterpreted.

A. Creation Revelation in Testimony of the Creation

According to David in Psalm 19,

> The heavens declare the glory of God,
>   and the sky above proclaims his handiwork.
> Day to day pours out speech,
>   and night to night reveals knowledge.
> There is no speech, nor are there words,
>   whose voice is not heard.
> Their voice goes out through all the earth,

---

[1] A covenant is a formalized relationship between multiple parties. A covenant is often companied by an oath to follow written or spoken parameters that outline the covenant, but this is not always present. A Christian marriage is a contemporary example of a covenant.

and their words to the end of the world. (vv. 1-4)

Clearly there is something about the created order that testifies to God in such a way that brings him glory and leads an observer to praise him.

It is necessary for us to consider how it does this and, if it is so clear, why so many people appear to miss it, why they do not believe in God. We saw in early chapters that Modernity thought knowledge was objective, independent of the one knowing. We also saw that Modernity was wrong on this count: the world we observe does not offer us truth apart from an interpretation. Realizing that truth is the combination of the observed world interpreted by an individual through an appropriate **worldview**, leading to a true interpretation, helps us answer these questions.

Applying these observations to creation, we can say that God's revelation in nature is a combination of objects that testify to his glory and an interpretation that recognizes these objects for what they are, testimonies to his glory. It is evident that a rock does not have letters inscribed on its side reading, "GOD CREATED ME." Yet when I walk along the beach near my home in Vancouver, I can't help but praise God as I pick up rocks and admire their many colours and unique features. A rock is something beautiful, and when I interpret it for what it truly is—a product of God's ingenuity—I see that its beauty reflects the beautiful glory of Yahweh, its Creator.

Creation is glorious. It is complex and beautiful. If we see this beauty within a worldview that recognizes God as the creator of these beautiful things, we identify this created glory as a reflection of he who is truly glorious. But if our worldview deliberately suppresses this truth, the created glory is taken as an end to itself. It becomes an object of worship instead of something pointing beyond itself. It is this exchange, of the Creator for his creature, that led Carl Sagan to write,

> In its encounter with Nature, science invariably elicits a sense of reverence and awe. The very act of understanding is a celebration of joining, merging, even if on a very modest scale, with the magnificence of the Cosmos.[2]

When the Creator is rejected, his very attributes attested to in creation are

---

[2] Carl Sagan, *The Demon-Haunted World: Science as a Candle in the Dark*, 1st Ed. (New York: Ballantine Books, 1997), 29..

attributed to the creature, in this case, "the Cosmos." Though it is perverted by human rebellion, creation should lead us to glorify God. God has not, however, left us only with a testimony to what is. He has also revealed in creation the appropriate way to act within and towards it.

B. Creation Revelation in the Morality of the Created Order

Creation revelation does not fulfil its function if it only shows us what is—that Yahweh exists—and not what we ought to do about this truth. Romans 1:18-32 does not just say that humans know God from the creation; it says that we are all held guilty for rebelling against God's revelation in creation. Part of this revelation, then, is the revelation of how we are to respond to the revelation of God's character in creation.

This revelation cannot stop there, however, for after listing all the sins that result from their disordered worship, Paul says that all humans have known "God's righteous decree," that these things are wrong and are deserving of condemnation (Rom 1:32). This explains why several times in this chapter Paul identifies some sinful actions as contrary to nature, contrary to the created order (e.g. v. 26, cf. 1 Cor 11:14). Paul affirms this in Romans 2:12-16 when he writes that the gentiles, who have not received the Law (the covenantal legislation in the books of Moses, Genesis-Deuteronomy), demonstrate by their works that they know the law (God's created legislation). They show that they know this law, yet he says that their discernment of it—their conscience—is confused, giving a conflicting account (Rom 2:15). What we see is that God has given to human beings revelation not only of the appropriate interpretation of the created world but also of the appropriate response they should take to God's creation.

As we noted in the last section, this created moral sense is covenantal. God has granted every human knowledge of the law governing his covenant with creation—the covenant he enacted with all humans in the first chapters of Genesis (Genesis 1-3, then Genesis 9). We have all, however, exchanged the truth of God for a lie and therefore exchanged his moral standard for our own. This moral revelation is corrupted by human rebellion, leading to even further sin. We could identify this revelation as discernment. This moral revelation is the knowledge necessary to determine the appropriate response to God's revelation in creation, to the world as rightly interpreted through the Christian worldview. It is closely tied to the objective side of revelation, the created world, and to the subjective side, the human interpretive faculties. This subjective side is what remains for us to consider.

C. Creation Revelation in Human Faculties

We saw in the first section of this book that knowledge is not purely objective, something found independently of an interpreting mind. For this reason, our account of created revelation must take both the subjective and objective sides of knowledge into account. We have already considered the objective side, those things being interpreted, so now we consider an area of created revelation not always addressed, human faculties (i.e. the senses and mind).

If created objects and the events in which they are involved testify to God's existence and character, it is because they are interpreted in a way appropriate to their actual nature: they have a quality—let's call it "createdness"—that testifies to God and need to be interpreted by a worldview that recognizes such a category. When Romans 1:25 tells us that all human beings have exchanged the truth of God for a lie, it is not telling us they have exchanged objects that testify to God for objects that do not. No, they have traded the appropriate interpretation of the created order for one that perverts its true nature. The creation was made by God, but they consider it uncreated. It points to the glory of God, but they identify this glory as a property of the creation and not its Creator.

That we can recognize God in the created order (even though we all at first reject him) reveals that we all are born with the appropriate interpretive grid for interpreting creation. This is obvious at one level, God created us with minds to understand, ears to hear, and eyes to see. He has given men and women the appropriate physical tools necessary to interpret the created order. These are necessary parts of God's created revelation, giving us the physical capacity to interact with it. But God must have granted humans something else to interpret the data received from our senses appropriately.

I do not mean the astounding ways our brain interprets light signals so that we see a picture—amazing as that is—but the mental software, the worldview, that allows us to take that picture and give it meaning. Consider a bee; it is not enough for us to see it in order to interact with it. To identify it, to know how to respond to it, we must have the appropriate pieces of data in place already. We must have something philosophers call **innate ideas**, fundamental assumptions that allow us to interpret the world but cannot be learned directly from the world. These ideas are needed before we can even begin to interpret the world.[3]

Part of created revelation, then, are important aspects of what we have been calling the Christian worldview, the interpretive beliefs necessary to look at the created world, give glory to Yahweh for it, and to then act in worshipful submission towards him. This involves the beliefs that God exists, that he is the Creator, that he is good, that he is faithful (and so **the law of non-contradiction,** see above), etc. However, if God has given humanity the necessary worldview to recognize and obey him from their birth, we must explain why many deny his existence and most do not follow him.

God has given humans the necessary interpretive framework to interpret the world and to recognize and worship him, yet humans have intentionally repudiated this gift and adopted a lie. In the words of Romans 1:18, we all "by [our] unrighteousness suppress the truth." Furthermore, according to Romans 8:6-7, the sinful mind cannot obey God. Romans 2:15 testifies to the confused conscience of human beings. We see, therefore, that the human mind has been corrupted by the Curse. Furthermore, the Curse has subjected our bodies to futility with the rest of the creation (cf. Rom 8:20), so none of our minds functions ideally. Yet this futility is not the fundamental problem that causes us to deny God and his commands.

The primary reason that humans fail to interpret creation correctly is that we are in rebellion against God. We suppress his truth and proceed to build an interpretive framework—a worldview—apart from the basic assumptions of his character and creating action. It is this denial of the right worldview that ultimately leads to the epistemological crisis we find ourselves in today. Our society's intellectual problems, then, are primarily moral problems. Therefore, salvation is as much about the salvation of our minds as it is about our souls. Because our epistemological problem is ultimately a moral problem, we need God's intervention—we need God's Word—to fix it.

Further Reading

---

[3] We talked a bit about innate ideas in ch. 2 and will again in ch. 10.

John Frame, *Systematic Theology*
John Frame, *The Doctrine of the Word of God*

On the Contribution of Objects

It may be worth nuancing the discussion thus far, for Immanuel Kant went a similar direction in his philosophy as I have in this book. However, there are many important distinctions between the approach I have taken and that of Kant.

For Kant, objects had a role to play in knowledge, yet they were ultimately unknowable. That is, at the other end of all experience was a *something*, yet this something was content-less—unknowable. Consider a tree, for example; according to Kant, everything you know about the tree is an imposition of the mind. The tree in itself is only the thing that furnishes an opportunity for knowledge. The problem is this: if knowledge is dependent on the interpreting subject, if there is no knowledge of an object apart from an interpretation, how does the object have *any* influence on knowledge. If shape, colour, smell, sound, etc. are all interpretations of the mind, how can I know what object stands behind these mental interpretations. Ultimately, this "object" is an unknowable entity, the only function of which is to provide an opportunity for experience. In fact, because the object only serves as an opportunity for knowing and contributes nothing to knowledge, it is hard to justify its existence: why should we even say that objects exist outside the mind?

This is an unacceptable conclusion for the Christian, yet it is hard to identify how exactly the object contributes to knowledge—what part it plays in our interpretation of it. On the one hand, we must say that some interpretations of an object are true or false, that the same object cannot be both a tree and a bee, yet it is hard to identify how the object itself is compatible or incompatible with either interpretation. I think, though, that we can tweak the standard illustration of Kant's thought for the role objects play in interpretation and furnish another illustration.

The epistemology of Immanuel Kant is often illustrated with a sausage machine, the machine which presses a formless mass of meat into the shape of a sausage. For Kant, the machine itself is the aspect of the human mind that brings unity to knowledge. An object sends out a signal, a packet of data, which Kant called a *percept*. This percept does not convey any information, instead it is "pressed" through the sausage machine and takes the shape of the mold. The mold of the machine is the innate categories of the human mind—shape, size, smell, taste, purpose, etc. Thus, we automatically take the formless *percept*—the mass of sausage meat—and press it through the mold of our mind, producing sense experience—a formed tube of sausage.

I have argued that our mind has a mold of sorts—it furnishes an interpretation of objects. Yet we cannot say that objects only furnish the opportunity for interpretation; we must account for their contribution to an interpretation, how they can be rightly or wrongly interpreted. Of course, the ultimate standard for interpretation is God's interpretation of the object, yet it is still an interpretation of *an object*. I suggest that we can illustrate the contribution of the object not with a sausage machine—which receives a formless mass of meat—but with two different illustrations.

First, we can illustrate it with a specific children's toy. You may remember from your childhood a toy that I have seen on many occasions, sometimes called a shape and sort. Basically, it is a box with several holes, often colour coded, with matching geometrical blocks—red and blue squares, blue rectangles, green circles, etc. The point of the toy is to match the coloured shape with the appropriate hole. In this analogy, innate ideas form the holes and colours. The data we receive from objects are the coloured shapes. The object suits some holes and not others. A large rock, for example, does not fit into the same hole as a small rock. Our mind functions to marry the proper shapes with the appropriate holes, producing knowledge. If we mismatch the shapes, we lose something in the process—forcing a cube through the circle will shave off parts and sticking the sphere through the cube will over-interpret the sphere. Knowledge only results when the data is put through a hole, yet the data is appropriate to one hole and does not suit another one. This pictures to some extent one aspect of interpretation, the recognition of empirical quantities—shape, size, colour, etc.

However, it is not appropriate for explaining non-empirical quantities such as meaning, value, and category or relation (e.g. "dog," "cat"), each of which are furnished by an individual's interpretative framework or worldview. In these cases, the object itself does not contribute to our interpretation; our worldview is solely responsible for these values. For example, the act of punching out a co-worker is not in itself right or wrong. It only acquires rightness or wrongness when we relate this act to a network of beliefs about right and wrong and to other pieces of data about the context of the action. The standard for this aspect of interpretation is not measured by the object but by the normative worldview, God's worldview. The accuracy of our interpretation in this regard is dependent upon the accuracy of our worldview and our consistency with it. Thus, we judge interpretation in this sense by measuring our worldview against God's revelation to determine its accuracy and we rely upon reference to the interpretations of others living out this worldview (primarily those recorded in the Bible but also of our peers and those recorded in history) to determine our consistency with it.

Second, we can illustrate the relation of our interpretation to its object by considering a painting. When an artist paints a forest, for example, he does not provide an exact replica of the object. Instead, he offers a particular perspective—an interpretation—of it. He has to be selective in what he includes and excludes; he labours to present a 3D object on a 2D medium. Depending on his purpose, he will shape the painting in one way or another—presenting lighting and such to elicit a specific reaction from the viewer. The point is this: when an artist creates a painting, he interprets the object by intentionally excluding some details, including others, and presenting the whole in a specific way. The end result bears a definite resemblance to but is clearly not the object itself.[i]

In this same way, our mental interpretation of an object is like a painter's painting; it shapes the raw data into a representation of the object that resembles yet is not identical to the object of interpretation. Thus, when two people have knowledge of the same object, their interpretation should resemble one another's because they are interpreting the same object. Yet because there is a subjective element—their particular physical and mental line-of-sight—their interpretations will not be identical. Even those with the same worldview will see and so interpret objects in slightly different ways. In this case, learning the from the interpretation of others can enrich our understanding of the objects we interpret. On this point, see the excursus in Chapter 2 on multi-perspectivalism.

[i] This illustration is dependent on the work of my Old Testament teacher, V. Philips Long. See especially his book *The Art of Biblical History*.

6

THE COVENANTAL REVELATION OF GOD'S SPEECH

Your word is a lamp to my feet
>   and a light to my path. – Psalm 119:105

Trading the truth for a lie has left humanity in a precarious place. We are continually progressing in knowledge and understanding, yet every day the assumptions that make such progress possible are being eroded. A moral standard that would lead a researcher to prioritize truth over money is no longer acknowledged. Faith in the objectivity of knowledge has been lost, and it is more clear each passing day that no real foundation remains for the sweeping truth claims of philosophy and science. In fact, in materialistic philosophy and science, it is considered legitimate to ask if we are only a computer simulation. Some philosophers and scientists answer "probably" and advise that it really may not be so bad to be someone else's computer program:

> "Maybe we're in a simulation, maybe we're not, but if we are, hey, it's not so bad," says David Chalmers.
> "My advice is to go out and do really interesting things," says Max Tegmark, "so the simulators don't shut you down."[1]

---

[1] Chalmers, a philosopher, and Tegmark, a cosmologist, are quoted in a Scientific America article on the debate over the reality of our experience. https://www.scientificamerican.com/article/are-we-living-in-a-computer-simulation/.

If we begin with ourselves as the starting point and ultimate authority for knowing, this is a legitimate, if not the most reasonable, conclusion to draw. The perverse exchange of the truth of God for the lie of human autonomy—that we do not need him and would be better off on our own—leads to these conclusions. This makes sense: if the world is created and governed by God, to think about it apart from him will have catastrophic conclusions.

This hit home for me about ten years ago, after watching the Matrix for the umpteenth time. Lying in bed long into the night, I pondered what it would be like for one of those characters living in the Matrix. How would they know their world was a lie? With a growing sense of discomfort, I could not think of a way they could. I could not figure out a way I could prove I was not in such a simulation.

Considering my senses, I pondered the possibility that they were part of a carefully written program to give the illusion of sense. Assuming that my mind was the final standard of truth and reasoning from my experience, I could not prove with logic that anything outside of myself existed—let alone that I was not a program! Would not a computer program granted self-awareness feel just like I had most of my life? Programmed to believe the experiences flitting through its brain, it would recognize its experience as normal and the truth. At the point of tears, I considered the only way to know that this was not the case, to know that my senses were trustworthy and that I was accurately interpreting my experience.

In the Matrix, it took those from outside, who knew the lie, to enter into the programmed world and offer a different perspective, a different **worldview**. Morpheus confronts Neo with a series of observations, odd things he had always noticed yet never could quite explain, and provides the interpretive key. These things did not make sense because he was not looking at them with the right interpretive lens; he was not considering his world as a computer program.

It dawned on me that night, as I opened my Bible and began to read Genesis 1, that the situation was not nearly as hopeless as I had imagined it to be. As Neo was not left on his own to figure out the lie, I was not left on my own to find confidence in the truth. I was assuming that it was my job to figure the world out, that I was the absolute authority and could trust nothing else but myself. I had bought into the lie of human autonomy. This was not the world the Bible presents, the world created by Yahweh. He created the universe and did not leave himself without a witness. He gave humanity the interpretive faculties to make sense of his world.

When we all fell into sin with Adam, our first parent, Yahweh graciously condescended to speak to his sinful creatures and reveal the truth. God spoke and corrected the lie into which we bought. Without a voice from the outside, we would truly be doomed to a hopeless scepticism. Yet we are not without such a voice. God, in a tremendous act of mercy, has spoken. He has spoken clearly and given us all we need to know him and act rightly before him. While we were lost in the darkness, blindly feeling around for some sort of guide, God provided us with a lamp for our feet. He provided for us light to make clear the path before us (Psalm 119:105).

All our knowledge problems began with rebellion against God, so the solution he provided to this rebellion will provide a solution to our knowledge problems. God has acted since the Fall to bring salvation to his people, to redeem a people for himself from among his rebellious creation. Beginning with Eve and her children, God enacted a plan to bring about the defeat of sin and death and deliver sinners from his righteous wrath against their sin. Beginning with Noah, Abraham, and then Israel, he brought this plan to climactic fruition in Jesus Christ his Son. Through his life, death, and resurrection, Jesus established a way for sinners to be made right with God. He instituted a New Covenant, a new way that humans could relate to their God.

With this **covenant** came a document, a book by which those in covenant with Jesus could know him and how to fulfil his will on earth as they await his return. His life, death and resurrection dealt with our relationship problem, reconciling us to God from whom we were estranged. What remained to be repaired was our knowledge problem. Scripture does not only tell us the good news that Salvation is available in Jesus Christ; it is a covenant document given to legislate God's covenant with us. It is given to repair our rebellious worldview so that we might properly interpret and act within God's world to achieve his purposes.[2]

---

[2] I unpack this, that Scripture is a covenant document and how to read it as such, in the next volume of this series, *The Gift of Reading Part 1 & 2*.

The Scriptures are given as our primary interpretive key to reality. It presents the Christian worldview so that we can rightly interpret creation and act appropriately within it. God's Word not only tells us about himself and how to follow him, it also tells us everything we need to know about the world he has made so that we can function faithfully within it.

Scripture, to function in this capacity, has properties theologians call authority and inerrancy, sufficiency, and clarity. In other words, Scripture is absolutely true and our final authority. Scripture is sufficient so that we can interpret and act appropriately within God's creation. Finally, Scripture is clear so that we can use it for its intended purposes, so that we might be equipped for everything God has asked of us. For the rest of this chapter, I want to look closer at these properties, seeing how God has provided us in Scripture the answers necessary to make sense of our confused world.

A. The Authority and Inerrancy of Scripture

But, YHWH is in his holy temple,
   be silent before him all the earth! – Habakkuk 2:20

Authority is ultimately the question of whom we trust. It is the question do we trust ourselves or God? It should be obvious that if God exists, he is the ultimate authority for his creation. As his Word, Scripture bears final authority, authority to govern our thoughts and our interpretations, to tell us how we should act and feel. Biblical authority means that Scripture's words are God's words and so our final standard for interpreting creation and acting within it. By calling the Bible authoritative, we are affirming with all the writers of Scripture that the Bible carries *God's* authority.

That the Bible is authoritative is evident from practically every page of Scripture. It is evident that God the creator and interpreter of all reality is the ultimate authority; therefore, anything He says is authoritative. 2 Timothy 3:16-17 says that all Scripture was breathed out by God, that is, it is his words. Paul here refers specifically to the Old Testament with which Timothy was raised, but Peter goes on to lump Paul's letters into this same category— *inspired* Scripture (2 Pet 3:15-16). The Scriptures are all those books God has given to govern his people in their covenant with him and so encompasses both the Old and New Testaments. All of these books are breathed out by

God, his very words.

Peter also says, earlier in 2 Peter, that no prophecy found in Scripture is of the prophet's own interpretation but of the Spirit (2 Pet 1:20-21). (Prophecy refers to all of Scripture, not just texts with messages about the future.) The author of Hebrews also writes that "Long ago, at many times and in many ways, God spoke to our fathers by the prophets, ²but in these last days he has spoken to us by his Son, whom he appointed the heir of all things, through whom also he created the world" (Heb 1:1-2). God spoke through the prophets, and now has spoken through his Son and, by extension, those whom his Son commissioned (e.g. Gal 1:12).

Some of the Old Testament records the historical speech of God, and when the prophets speak, it is difficult to distinguish between their speech and God's, so close is the connection. But the Bible repeatedly claims that *every* Biblical text, even the Psalms—not just direct speech and the prophets—are spoken by God. The authors, such as David or the prophets, are identified as his means of speaking: for example, "*saying through David* so long afterward... 'Today, if you hear his voice'....⁸For if Joshua had given them rest, *God would not have spoken* of another day" (Heb 4:7-8, emphasis added); "God spoke by the mouth of his holy prophets long ago" (Acts 3:21, cf. Luke 1:70) (cf. Mark 12:36; Acts 1:16, 4:25, 28:25).

Therefore, when we say, "the Scriptures are authoritative," we mean "The Scriptures, as the very words of God, bear his authority." The writers of Scripture are analogous—and this is a very near analogy—to the letter bearers or heralds of a great king. When heralds come to the king's subjects with a message (whether they paraphrase his words or read his words exactly), they come with his authority. Rejecting the words of the king's messengers is a rejection of the words of the king. Spurning the messengers is an insult to him. Doing so would incur the wrath of a king (cf. Matt 21:33-22:14). God is our great king, the King of kings. To reject the prophets of God and their message is to reject God himself (cf. Acts 8:51). As God's very words, the Holy Scriptures are therefore completely authoritative and demand the obedience of all of God's creation.

The authority of God, and so Scripture is ultimate: he is the creator and has unquestionable rights and authority (cf. Job 38-41; Rom 9:15, 20-21), God is also our covenant Lord. He has the authority to give commands, expect obedience, and pour out wrath upon the disobedient, as is attested throughout Scripture. The Bible, then, as God's very words, carries this same authority. This identity between God and his words is so close that David, in Psalm 56, speaks several times about praising God's word (56:4, 10-11). Because Scripture is authoritative in this ultimate sense, we must also maintain that it is inerrant, free from error. Though it may appear as though I have tried to pull a fast one, covering two points under one heading, we must see that inerrancy is not a separate issue from authority. The inerrancy of Scripture is essential to the claim that the Bible is our authority.

If Scripture is God's word, it is trustworthy and inerrant both because God is trustworthy and inerrant (cf. Ps 56, Rom 11:33-36, etc.) *and* because it is absolutely authoritative. That is, if Scripture is absolutely authoritative—bearing God's own authority—it can never be in error, for there is no authority qualified to tell us it is wrong. Think about it: if we wanted to prove God wrong, where would we go? Would we turn to science? Yahweh created the world and all that is in it. He would tell us that we are wrong, maybe tell us the reason we are wrong—perhaps not—and command us to submit (cf. Job 38-41, Hab 2:20).

Would we turn to experience? Yahweh would remind us,

> He who planted the ear, does he not hear?
> He who formed the eye, does he not see? (Ps 94:9)

Or he might say, "But who are you, O man, to answer back to God?" (Rom 9:20). Patiently, he might just lay bare our finitude. He might tell us that we cannot rightly interpret our experience unless we know ourselves perfectly. We cannot even evaluate what is going on in the deepest recesses of our heart and mind; we cannot see what biases are at play. Yet he who is completely omniscient knows the depths of our heart and everything else: how could we dare pit our finite understanding against the infinite depths of his wondrous knowledge. "Where you there," he might ask,

> when I laid the foundation of the earth?
>   Tell me, if you have understanding.
> Who determined its measurements—surely you know!
>   Or who stretched the line upon it?
> On what were its bases sunk,
>   or who laid its cornerstone,

> when the morning stars sang together
>   and all the sons of God shouted for joy?
>
> "Or who shut in the sea with doors
>   when it burst out from the womb,
> when I made clouds its garment
>   and thick darkness its swaddling band,
> and prescribed limits for it
>   and set bars and doors,
> and said, 'Thus far shall you come, and no farther,
>   and here shall your proud waves be stayed'?
>
> Have you commanded the morning since your days began,
>   and caused the dawn to know its place? (Job 38:4-12)

There is nothing in all creation that has the authority to tell the Creator that he is wrong. In the Christian worldview, only God and his creation exist; therefore, God has unquestionable authority. If Scripture is God's words, as it claims throughout, then there is nothing with the authority to show that it is wrong. It, therefore, must be inerrant—something it happily claims for itself (e.g. Isa 40:8; Ps 19:7, 8, 9; 119:43, 89-90, 127-128, 138-140, 151-152, 160, 163; Matt 5:17-18; 24:35; Luke 16:17; John 10:35; 17:17).

This question of authority is what the epistemological crisis of our age finally comes down to: do we trust in the creature or the Creator? We are born trusting ourselves, and this leads us headlong into one disaster after another. It is only by God's gracious mercy that we are not successful in our suppression of his truth. But he has not left us in this state. He has not left us with only a glimmer of light amidst endless darkness. With boundless grace he has entered his creation and made himself known, saving us first from our sinful rebellion and the wrath we deserved on account of it but also from the hopelessness of living without God in his world. Scripture, the solution to our problem of knowledge, is truly a gracious gift.

God has given us a word that we can trust, a word that tells us we can trust our senses, trust our minds, and tells us how we can know him and his world. By freeing us from the trap of human autonomy, his authoritative Word allows us to gain our footing and begin the task of knowing. But knowing that God is our authority and that he has made himself known in Scripture is only helpful in as much as what he has revealed is sufficient for the task at hand.

B. The Sufficiency of Scripture

> All Scripture is breathed out by God and profitable for teaching, for reproof, for correction, and for training in righteousness, that the man of God may be complete, equipped for every good work. – 2 Timothy 3:16-17

Many today claim that Scripture is indeed sufficient, that it is all that is necessary *to accomplish its purpose*, yet they would define that purpose very narrowly. Scripture, some claim, tells us about God and how to obey him, but it does not answer any of the sorts of questions science and philosophy answer.

If this were true, we would be in serious trouble—as I believe we have seen so far. Scripture, in contrast to this contemporary idea, does not so limit itself. The key text for our consideration here is 2 Timothy 3:16-17. Paul writes that all Scripture is spoken by God and so is useful, with the result that God's people might be "equipped for every good work." Some theologians take this narrowly, suggesting that it gives us sufficient "religious" knowledge for following God. Let us consider for a moment, however, what is necessary if we are to be ready for "every good work."

We obviously need to know what works God would have us to do, yet this is not enough. Good works in the Bible are only good in as much as they come from a heart set on God (Luke 6:43-45; Rom 8:6-8; Heb 11:6); therefore, the Bible needs also be sufficient to tell us about God, the Gospel, and the need for faith. Good works need more than this though: to be able to act towards others and the creation in a way appropriate to God's will, we need to be sure that they actually exist. We need to know that we can trust our interpretation of them, that the sense-data coming from eyes and hands is valid, and that the logic we use to apply Scriptural teachings to real-life situations is valid.

Furthermore, if we are to do good works with our eyes set on eternity, we need to know that history will progress and this creation will come to an end at Christ's return. That may not sound significant, yet many religions and philosophies teach that history is a cycle (i.e. it repeats itself for eternity). Indeed, we need to know that history is linear, that it progresses in a straightforward manner, and that the past actually happened if we are to believe that Jesus rose from the dead (cf. 1 Cor 15). These are all areas under contention in the areas of philosophy known as metaphysics, which addresses questions about reality or existence, and **epistemology**. The Bible must provide some answers to such questions, or we will not be adequately equipped for every good work.

When we look at the teaching of Scripture, it is clear that it tells us more than what to do (ethics) and whom we love and serve (the doctrine of God); it tells us how the world began, where it is going, and how we can be sure of what we know. We will consider what the Bible says about logic and our senses in the last section of this book, but observe with me that the Bible is not shy about talking of issues that philosophy and science also discuss (though it addresses them in a very different manner). Philosophy and some fields of science are very interested in the origins of the world, so is Scripture (Gen 1-3, Job 38, etc.). The Philosophy of history considers whether history began and will have an end or will continue in a cyclical fashion; these concerns are addressed by the Biblical authors for various purposes (Heb 9:25-28; 10:1-4, 11-14; 2 Pet 3:1-10). Philosophers also speculate on the different types of existence. The Bible gives us two categories: everything that exists is either the Creator or a creature. History asks many things about historical events which the Bible also discuss, e.g. the life and death of Jesus; the falls of Israel, Assyria, Judah, and Babylon; etc.[3]

Scripture speaks of all these things, and it does so with God's authority. Jesus asked Nicodemus, "If I have told you earthly things and you do not believe, how can you believe if I tell you heavenly things?" (John 3:12) The Bible is as authoritative when it tells us about history and truth as it is when it speaks of Jesus and God the Father. Scripture is authoritative in these areas and tells us about such areas so that we might be equipped for every good work.

The Bible gives us sufficient knowledge of God and his will for us, and it repairs the worldview twisted by our rebellion. Scripture gives us sufficient knowledge of God and his created world to appropriately interpret it, glorify

---

[3] For more on how the Bible answers the questions of metaphysics, Volume 3, *The Gift of Seeing*.

him in response to this interpretation, and act appropriately within it. Scripture is sufficient, yet sufficiency only helps us if Scripture is clear enough for us to understand its sufficient content.

C. The Clarity of Scripture

> Your word is a lamp to my feet
> and a light to my path. – Psalm 119:105

"In a word: if Scripture is obscure or [ambiguous]," wrote Martin Luther,

> why need it have been brought down to us by act of God? Surely we have enough obscurity and uncertainty within ourselves, without our obscurity and uncertainty and darkness being augmented from heaven! And how then shall the apostle's word stand: "All Scripture is given by inspiration of God, and is profitable for doctrine, for reproof, for correction?" (2 Tim 3:16).[4]

For Martin Luther, the clarity of Scripture was a doctrine essential to the Christian faith. If God intended to give us a book that would reveal himself and his will for us, why would he make sloppy work of it and leave us a book that no one could understand? If *all* Scripture is useful, does this not also mean that all Scripture is clear, that it can be understood so that it is usable? In other words, if Scripture is a flashlight to illumine our paths, God must have given clear instructions for turning it on (cf. Ps 119:105).

A favourite text of Luther's was Deuteronomy 17:8. The people were commanded to bring their disputes before the priests who would discern the appropriate solution from the Law, "But how could they be settled if the laws were not perfectly clear, and were truly as lights among the people?"[5] The issue for Luther was twofold, and he is a wise guide in this matter. First, there is the issue of personal clarity: how can an individual Christian be sure that he or she is hearing God's voice in Scripture?

This question has been taken up by John Piper in recent years; he has

---

[4] Martin Luther, *The Bondage of the Will*, ed. J. I Packer and O. R Johnston (Grand Rapids: Fleming H. Revell, 2003), 128.

[5] Ibid., 125.

done a masterful job showing how the Scriptures testify to their divine inspiration. In John 10:27, Jesus says that his sheep hear his voice, that they are his and recognize him speaking. Piper argues that through the words of Scripture, God's glory is seen—much as creation testifies to his glory—and that the knowledge God has given all of us in creation is matched to this glorious testimony. If the Holy Spirit removes the blinders of our sin, we recognize the glory of God shining forth from the words he speaks:

> there is in every human being a 'knowledge' of this God. There is a built-in template that is shaped to receive as its perfect counterpart this peculiar communication of God's glory. When God opens our eyes (2 Cor. 4:6) and grants us the knowledge of the truth (2 Tim. 2:25), through the Scriptures (1 Pet. 1:23), we know that we have met ultimate reality. And in this way, God testifies that his word is true.[6]

Every Christian needs to be able to be sure of the Divine authority of Scripture we have talked about, and not all can go through the detailed philosophical and historical arguments made for it. The personal clarity of Scripture answers this: God attests to the humble regenerate reader that this is indeed his word. His sheep hear his voice and recognize him.

Scripture cannot only possess clarity in this sense, however, for it is meant to be taught and to govern the public behaviour of Christians—not only their private thoughts. Scripture, if it is to function authoritatively as Scripture, cannot be slippery and ambiguous, unusable. Martin Luther argued vigorously that it also possesses an external, public clarity. Scripture is clear in the words with which it communicates so that Christians can settle disagreements by turning to Scripture (e.g. Deut 17:8). Scripture presupposes this sense of clarity when it commends the Bereans for "examining the Scriptures daily to see if these things were so" (Acts 17:11-12). It also assumes this in the expectation that parents will teach their children the Law (Deut 6:1-9; cf. 2 Tim 3:10-17), that young men can meditate on the words of Scripture and keep themselves pure (Ps 119:9-11; cf. Josh 1:8), and that elders or pastors can hold fast and teach the word (1 Tim 4:12-16, 6:2-5; 2 Tim 4:1-2).

---

[6] John Piper, *A Peculiar Glory: How the Christian Scriptures Reveal Their Complete Truthfulness* (Wheaton: Crossway, 2016), 226.

If Scripture is useful to equip us for every good work, then it must be understandable, clear. Yet it need not be understandable to the same degree for everyone. That is, Luther would not deny that applying Scripture to everyday life is at times difficult; Scripture does not deny this either. In fact, Peter writes of some hard to understand things in Paul's writing, "which the ignorant and unstable twist to their own destruction, as they do the other Scriptures" (2 Pet 3:16). It is clear that he does not see all of Paul's writings as equally clear, yet those who are led astray are not considered positively either. They are "lawless people" in addition to being ignorant and unstable (v. 17).

That not all Scripture is equally clear is evident to those of us who read the Biblical languages: though smoothed out by English translations, Acts 27 and the book of Hebrews are harder to read or translate than the Gospel of John or even Romans. As with our discussion of creation revelation, the clarity of the Biblical text is partly a feature of the text and partly a feature of what we bring to the text. In 1 Corinthians 2:9-16, Paul writes that those who do not have the Spirit cannot understand the Word of God, because it is folly to them (cf. Rom 8:6-8). But Christians have been given the Spirit and can properly understand the Scriptures because they have the author with them (cf. Rom 8:4-6, 9). So part of this is the proper understanding of God and the Scriptures as directed by the Spirit, yet the physical text must also be clear if this interpretive lens is to yield any fruit.[7]

We can make a further clarification, though, for it is clear that not all Christians are at the same reading level or able to understand the same types of speech (e.g. academic vs. colloquial). A child, for example, may not be able to understand a passage of Scripture that another believer is perfectly capable of understanding. Yet a child will not need to wrestle with the same depth of thought as an adult may have to, so we can affirm that the relationship between Scripture's clarity and usefulness varies from person to person. I think it is reasonable to conclude that it is clear enough for all that God would have that person use it for. Furthermore, God has intended Scripture to be read and understood in Christian community, so where one person is lacking

---

[7] For more on the clarity of Scripture and how we interpret it, see the second volume in this series, *The Gift of Reading*.

God provides another so that they might understand his will for them revealed in Scripture (cf. Rom 12:3-8, 1 Cor 12:12-31, Eph 4:11-16).

From the teachings of Scripture then, we can say that all of God's Word is clear so as to be useful for his people and so that reasonable discussion can be conducted over the meaning and application of passages (cf. Deut 17:8; Acts 17:11-12).[8] The clarity of Scripture is in large part due to its self-interpreting nature; it is sufficient in breadth to provide in some areas key ideas that are useful for interpreting more difficult texts elsewhere (e.g. interpreting Hab 2:4 in light of Gen 15:6 and Lev 18:6, with Rom 1:17, Gal 3:11, and Heb 10:38).

The clarity of Scripture, then, means that the Scriptures speak clearly with God's voice so that his sheep may recognize him speaking. The same knowledge and spiritual illumination that allows us to recognize God's glory in Scripture equips the believer to understand the Scriptures by reading all the parts of Scripture in light of other parts and the teaching of the whole. Scripture is also sufficient to equip all believers for every good work God would ask of them in this life, its clarity enabling them to understand and so use its teaching. Finally, Scripture is God's very voice and so bears his authority. It is, therefore, without error in its clear communication of all God would have us know for living before him in the world he created.

Further Reading

B. B. Warfield, "Inspiration" (in, *Selected Shorter Writings of Benjamin B. Warfield*, vol. 1). [B]
Francis Schaeffer, *The Great Evangelical Disaster*. [B]
John Calvin, *The Institutes of the Christian Religion*, Book 1, Chs 6-9. [B-I]
John Frame, *Apologetics: A Justification of Christian Belief*. [B]
* John Frame, *The Doctrine of the Word of God*. [I]
John Frame, *Systematic Theology*, 519-693. [B-I]
* John Piper, *A Peculiar Glory*. [B]
* Martin Luther, *The Bondage of the Will*, 124-129. [I]

---

[8] I take the clarity of Scripture to imply that God's Word is clear enough in the original languages so that one knowledgeable in them may teach from the original languages and translate the Word clearly so that it can be used by those without access to the languages.

Wayne Grudem, *Systematic Theology*, 47-138. [B]

7

THE ETHICS OF KNOWING

> For the wrath of God is revealed from heaven against all ungodliness and unrighteousness of men, who by their unrighteousness suppress the truth. – Romans 1:18

We have seen so far that knowledge is a right interpretation of the world and the one who created it, an interpretation that corresponds to God's interpretation of his creation and himself. Truth, then, can be defined as any knowledge that corresponds to God's knowledge and contains no error. This implies something we may not usually think about. If truth intimately involves God and the knowledge he has revealed, then knowing is not only a mental activity but also a moral activity.

Think about it for a moment; if truth is thinking God's thoughts after him, then the pursuit of truth must involve submission to and pursuit of God. Knowing is not merely thinking about something in a certain manner, but thinking about something in submission to God. To appropriately know something, we must surrender the illusion of our autonomy—the perceived right to define the world as we see fit—and accept what God says to be true. This moral aspect of knowledge is why the exchange of the truth for a lie in Romans 1:18 invites the wrath of God upon humanity and why it results in rampant depravity. Epistemological rebellion is moral rebellion. Ignorance and immorality go hand in hand.

In Romans 8, this comes out clearly: the "mind set on the flesh" does not obey God, in fact, it is unable to do so. Highlighting the thoughts of those in rebellion against God, Paul indicates that their thinking is unable to lead them to submit to God in right actions (8:6-9). Therefore, rebellious thought (having a mind of the sinful flesh) leads to rebellious action.

In John 12:40, John quotes Isaiah to explain Israel's rejection of Jesus's miracles. Why do they not believe? He identifies the root of unbelief as a hardened rebellious heart, if the Spirit changed their heart—gave them the gift of regeneration—"they [would] see with their eyes, and understand with their heart."[1] In 1 Corinthians 2, Paul writes,

> The natural person does not accept the things of the Spirit of God, for they are folly to him, and he is not able to understand them because they are spiritually discerned. The spiritual person judges all things, but is himself to be judged by no one. "For who has understood the mind of the Lord so as to instruct him?" But we have the mind of Christ. (1 Cor 2:14-16)

Therefore, humans need not only functioning brains to learn about God and his world, but they also need submissive hearts. The search for truth is as much a moral act as the question of the appropriate use of human sexuality.

This means that science, philosophy, sociology, and English—even math—are not amoral subjects in which the question of God and his existence can be shoved aside for the moment. To search for truth in these fields without consideration of the God who has revealed himself is to set oneself in opposition to God, in rebellion against him, and to doom the task to futility. No matter how many true insights are revealed, they will be shrouded in a cloud of error. Furthermore, whatever truth is found will not even be identified appropriately, for it will be considered within a **worldview** that deliberately suppresses the knowledge of God. We have seen already that there is indeed truth in non-Christian thought, yet this is not because of any great feat of understanding on their part. What truth is found is evidence of the graciousness of God in not allowing the human heart to pursue its rebellion to the fullest. This has several practical implications, but I want to bring this section of the book to a close with the consideration of two.

---

[1] "The arm of the Lord" to be revealed in context is Jesus Christ, God's power embodied in his suffering servant (Isa 53:1). The revealing of Jesus is God's regenerating act to empower sinful people to believe in him (Deut 30:6; Jer 31:30-33; Isa 54:13; John 3:1-8, 6:44-45).

First, we should not be surprised when the pursuit of knowledge without consideration of God—the pursuit of knowledge found in most North American Universities—repeatedly comes to atheistic and incoherent conclusions.

When the starting assumption is that God is inconsequential to human knowing, it is not surprising that God is irrelevant to or excluded from the so-called knowledge that results from all fields of study. Consider evolution: if someone seeks to explain the universe without the interference or revelation of God, is it surprising that the resulting picture is a world where God is uninvolved or merely relegated to the role of first cause (the one who started everything moving)?

If, however, God is the reference point for all knowledge—if his existence is essential to right knowing—then we can also expect that the results of such study will be incoherent. If someone considers the created order without a category of creation, without consideration of the one who created it and the way he did so, will not her conclusions be profoundly flawed? If someone studies human sexuality without the consideration of God who created sexuality, is it surprising that biological sex (male/female) is ignored and that all manner of human self-invention is invited?

We are not, however, without hope in this world. Accurately identifying the disease means that we can recognise and begin to administer the appropriate cure. If the problem we face is ethical rebellion, the exchange of truth for a lie resulting in all-out apostasy toward God and his wrath towards all men and women, then the answer is the Gospel.

The second practical implication of the ethical aspect of knowing is that we know the cure: the Gospel and the Bible that communicates it are the answer to our world's epistemic crisis.

The Gospel, the good news that Jesus Christ, the second person of the Trinity, entered his creation and lived the life we could not, died the death we all deserved, and was raised on the third day, is not merely about the salvation of our souls. The Gospel is what we need to hear if we are to be delivered from the wrath of God by the blood of his Son, but it is more than this. If we are to think rightly about God and his world, we need to be saved from our rebellion. If we are to act rightly before him and accomplish his purposes, we need the promise of his spirit to overcome our sin and submit ourselves to Jesus Christ. In a word, if we truly want to know God and his creation, we need to be sanctified. We need a wholesale transformation into the image of God the Son. We need to gaze upon the glory of God shining forth in the face of Jesus Christ as he is revealed in Scripture if we want truth (cf. 2 Cor 3:12-4:6).

Individually, we need to steep ourselves in God's Word and pursue him if we want truth. To know the truth and be set free, we need the Spirit and his sanctifying work (1 Cor 2:14-16); to receive the Spirit and be sanctified, we need the truth of God's Word (John 17:17, Rom 10:14-17). It is the gracious gift our Lord Jesus Christ that he began our epistemic salvation before we could even believe in him (Rom 5:6-8), that while we were still sinners, he died for us and sent his Spirit to draw us to himself (John 6:44-45). He has made known to us the truth by his grace and given us the gracious gift of his Scriptures so that we could grow in the knowledge of him and his word. To properly understand anything in this world, therefore, we need to labour in the study of God's word by the power of his Spirit (cf. Phil 2:12). The Gospel saves the souls and the minds of Christians, yet we are not the only ones in need of this salvation.

If we want to convince the world of the truth of God and his Scriptures, to see transformation in its values and beliefs, we need to preach the Gospel. The world will not know the truth unless they receive the eyes to see the world as God has created it. To do this, they need to hear the Gospel of Jesus Christ proclaimed by his people (Rom 10:14-17). The World needs the Gospel of Jesus Christ not only for their souls but also for their sciences. It is Jesus and his Word that will ultimately save us from our epistemological crisis, and God in his grace has made this salvation available to all us.

On Reading or the Possibility Thereof [i]

How then will they call on him in whom they have not believed? And how are they to believe in him of whom they have never heard? And how are they to hear without someone preaching? And how are they to preach unless they are sent? As it is written, "How beautiful are the feet of those who preach the good news!" But they have not all obeyed the gospel. For Isaiah says, "Lord, who has believed what he has heard from us?" So faith comes from hearing, and hearing through the word of Christ. – Romans 10:14-17

In the introduction to this book, we saw Fredrich Nietzsche's striking description of the present age we are in,

> What were we doing when we unchained this earth from its sun? Where is it moving to now? Where are we moving to? Away from all suns? Are we not continually falling? And backwards, sidewards, forwards, in all directions? Is there still an up and a down? Aren't we straying as though through an infinite nothing?

Such is the state of Western society; without moorings, it is as if we are straying through an infinite void with nothing but human preference and feeling for guidance. An area where this is strongly expressed is reading and communication. In grade school and universities, television and politics, even law and Christian theology, the ability of texts (such as this book, the Bible, or the American constitution) to communicate is cast into doubt. Speech, it is claimed, is malleable or plastic from the moment it leaves the mouth or pen of the author. That is, it is open to infinite interpretation as determined by the reader and his interaction with the text.

We must ask if this is really the inevitable conclusion we must draw from reasoned thought and experience; is this the way it has to be? The stakes are not small in this, for the Gospel comes through human communication, the word of God read or proclaimed (Rom 10:14-17). If texts cannot communicate, the Gospel cannot go forth.

I want to contend briefly that the interpretive chaos in which we find ourselves does not result from unclear texts or speech (for the most part) nor an unbridgeable hermeneutical gap (there is no chasm separating our minds from the world with which we interact) but a rejection of humanity as made in the image of God and God as **covenant** Lord over man. The answer to hermeneutical chaos is the Christian worldview, in which every person is obligated to honour the communicative intent of every other person, to the extent of their abilities, and is ultimately obligated to honour God's communicative intent in creation and His written revelation.

It is true that a text is unable to force the reader to properly interpret it—to follow the natural rules of reading—but this does not mean that interpretation is open ended or subjective. This only means that the onus is on the reader to adopt the appropriate posture for right interpretation. Reading is, in fact, contractual or covenantal. For most written works or spoken communication, this covenant is non-obligatory: most of us have taken a quote out of context for comedic purposes (in jest, I often adopt Luke's tortured face from Star Wars Episode V and exclaim to my wife, "Noooooooo!!! That's impossible!!!"). We recognize such twisting of words as a comedic effort; no one confuses such a play on meaning as a valid "interpretation" of the original.

To properly read a work, we must enter into an implicit agreement with the author, an agreement that we will, if possible, honour them by seeking to interpret their work on its own terms—in its context. This applies to written and spoken communication equally, though it is more evident in the latter because of the immediate consequences. Who has not felt the hurt or awkwardness when this communicative covenant is broken? Many times, my friends have chosen to take things I have said and strip them of their context, to give them a new interpretation—much to my horror! This is so effective because everyone recognizes that there is an intentional breach of the communicative covenant. This same agreement exists in written communication, only in this case there is only the reader to ensure their own fidelity to this relationship. Reading is thus a moral act—forcing us to choose whether we will honour another person or not—but one that usually has very little consequences (e.g. to misread a novel is to do no great harm).

Yet there are communications in which such covenant breaking is a weightier matter. In legal proceedings and business, much rests on honouring the communicative covenant. To break this agreement may entail the jailing of the innocent if their testimony is twisted, the freeing of the guilty, or the defrauding of many. In academic studies (other than among postmodern deconstructionist circles) a student is expected to accurately communicate the meaning of the work being analyzed. Grades, graduation, or academic probation rest on one's success or failure at such analysis. At a more significant level, communication from the government bears even greater weight. To break the communicative covenant with the law means fines or a prison sentence—even death!

However, none of these instances presents the greatest moral imperative to the reader. Our ultimate moral obligation is to God and all human beings are obligated to obey to his commands. This binds us on many levels to follow the communicative covenant. For all humanity, our first moral obligation is to uphold the communicative covenant God has established with creation. God has, according to Romans 1:18-32, revealed Himself clearly in His creation. Though they were obligated to receive this communication, this text tells us that all humanity breaks this covenant and exchanges the truth for a lie: they sin in misinterpretation. This communicative covenant exists for all God's words: all humans are morally compelled to appropriately interpret, believe and respond rightly to the Gospel proclamation. To fail in this is sin—rebellion against God.

Furthermore, The Bible is a covenant document from God and demands of its reader obedience in reading. As God's very words it demands interpretive obedience that is analogous to that of a federal constitution or royal proclamation, only to the utmost degree. If one dare not disobey and therefore misinterpret the constitution on penalty of law, or dare not misinterpret and disobey the command of one's king, how much more should one fear to do so concerning God?

The interpretive obligations imposed by God do not stop, however, with His own words: God not only binds us to communicative obedience with himself; He binds us in communicative obedience to others. That we are to submit to earthly authorities means that we are to appropriately interpret their words (cf. Rom 13, 1 Pet 2:13-17). That we are to honour others as image bearers of God and seek to uphold justice in our communication means that we are morally obligated to interpret their communication correctly. (This does not mean we cannot joke, only that such twisting of communication must be in a context where it is clear that the communicative intent is understood.) We are also obligated to interpret God's creation rightly, meaning that to ignore His revelation in creation is not ignorance but criminal negligence.

It is therefore the case that, though texts may not force us to obey their communicative intent as demonstrated by the directions they provide (context), God commands us to honour their communicative efforts. This implies, on the other hand, that authors are under obligation to ensure communicative accuracy, and are liable for breaking the communicative covenant on their end (of course, intended audience matters here).

[i]This excursus is adapted from a post I wrote on Teleioteti.ca. https://teleioteti.ca/2017/11/20/the-moral-act-of-reading-a-response-to-deconstructionism/.

Further Reading

John Frame, *The Doctrine of the Knowledge of God* [I]
John Frame, *The Doctrine of the Word of God* [I]

—PART 3—
THE PRACTICE OF EPISTEMOLOGY

8

CREATED IN THE IMAGE OF GOD: THINKING AS A CREATURE

> The secret things belong to the Lord our God, but the things that are revealed belong to us and to our children forever, that we may do all the words of this law.
> – Deuteronomy 29:29

In Part 1 of this book, we examined the nature of knowing itself, the delicate balance between the world outside of us and the interpretive software within us. In Part 2, we considered the fundamental role of authority in knowing and the role God's revelation plays in making knowing possible. In Part 3, we will consider our role as knowers. That is, we will consider how our senses, minds, and hearts work to make knowledge possible.

Having concluded the last chapter with the role of morality in knowing (with the human heart and its relation to God's authority), we will begin this part of the book with the same theme. We will answer the question "what should our attitude be as we seek to interpret God's world?" The Bible teaches that humans are creatures—the artful products of a Creator—and, therefore, that all our thinking must be done as creatures (cf. Rom 9:19-21; Eph 2:10). We have seen already that this means we must think in submission to God's revelation. In direct application to our thinking, I want to consider in this chapter how thinking as a creature means seeing God as the ultimate reference point for meaning and being aware of our finitude.

A. God is the Reference Point for Meaning

Let's begin with a question: does understanding God help us understand ourselves, or does self-understanding help us understand God? On one level, the answer is "both." John Calvin began his *Institutes of the Christian Religion* with the incredible insight that we can only know God by knowing ourselves as his creations and that we can only truly know ourselves by knowing God as our creator. If we were starting as a blank slate, this would be a hopeless circle—I could never know God or myself! Yet God has revealed himself in Scripture and given us knowledge of him from birth, so this circle of interpretation works well. Surely we have all experienced a growing understanding of God and his work as we begin to grasp more and more the depths of our sinfulness and the greatness of being made in his image! Calvin's insight is truly profound, but it is not the full story. The reason that self-knowledge helps us understand God is because he has created us in his image and created us to see him in his creation.

Unfortunately, the Fall means that this image is marred: no individual human or human relationship perfectly reflects God. If we believe that human experience is ultimate in explaining God, then we will be left with a distorted picture of the God we worship. For example, God has revealed himself as a Father. If we take the word "father" and define it from our experiences, we will horribly misunderstand God! All of us have had imperfect fathers. Some have been worse than others, but none have been a perfect father. If "father" means what I have experienced, then my view of God as Father will be impoverished. If "father" means the bigger, better version of the father figures we have experienced, then our understanding of God will still be too small. God's fatherhood embodies the best of what our earthly fathers have done, yet his fatherhood extends to so much more.

Therefore, it is crucial to recognize that our experiences of earthly fathers do not define God's fatherhood. The exact opposite is, in fact, the case. God is the perfect Father who has existed before any human counterpart. We only recognize good fathers as "good" in light of how they reflect God's perfect fatherhood. We only recognize bad fathers as "bad" in light of how they fail in comparison to the example God has given us. All of us know the invisible attributes of God from his created order (Rom 1:20), surely his fatherhood is included. We could say that God is the standard of what fatherhood should look like: we recognize as fathers those whose role corresponds to that which God has. We recognize someone as a good father when they act in their role the way God acts in that role. A bad father would be someone who does not act in his fatherhood as God does. This means that God is the reference point of meaning, the fixed standard by which we understand our experience. That God is the reference point for meaning requires a colossal paradigm shift in our thinking yet is tremendously important if we want to understand him properly.

This necessary shift in our thinking may be most evident if we consider the Biblical teaching that God does all He does for his glory. From Scripture, we learn that God created the world to display his glory (Gen 1:27-28; Isa 43:5-7; Pss 19:1, 72:19). God raises and deposes world leaders for this purpose (Isa 63:12; Hab 2:14; Rom 9:16-18), and works all things together according to a plan made before the foundations of the earth were laid to make known his character—to demonstrate his glory—to his elect creation (e.g. Isa 48:9-11; Rom 9:22-24; Eph 1:8-10). In Romans 1:18-32, the very act that brought the wrath of God against humanity is the exchange of his glory for that of the creature. If we try to understand this from the perspective of our experience, we are bound to think God is horrible!

When we think of those who pursue their own glory, the adjectives that come to mind are *proud, arrogant, selfish, sinful,* and *manipulative*. Is this how we are to think of God's actions? Are they the selfish actions of a maniacal tyrant? May it never be! If we start with the perspective of humans, we understand the pursuit of self-glory from the perspective of the perverted and vain pursuits of rebellious creatures. How, though, would God have us look at his pursuit of his own glory?

If we look to God to understand this, not our experience, it makes much more sense. The Bible teaches that God is worthy of our worship, of glory: God is infinitely beautiful and good, strong and wise, etc. Idolatry is roundly condemned as a sin because it is a horrible lie. That is, to commit idolatry is to take the good gifts of God and thank his creatures for them. Idolatry is taking the perfect character of God and attributing it to his creatures, thereby distorting and perverting his perfections to match the mangled mess of a creature we choose to worship. If it is idolatrous to attribute what is rightfully God's to his creatures, then God would be idolatrous to pursue anything other than his own glory. To do this would be to treat something that is not

God as God; this is something God cannot do. This, in fact, why the human pursuit of glory appears to us as wrong, because it involves exalting oneself to the place of God!

Another important aspect of God's pursuit of his glory taught by Scripture is that in this pursuit, humans find their greatest satisfaction. That is, God did not set out to manifest his glory in creation and create creatures who would hate this endeavour. God made humans with a desire for happiness, for fulfillment, and gave his own glory as the answer to this desire. So when God pursues his glory with his creatures, this should bring us the greatest happiness. John Piper has famously summarised this with the phrase, "God is most glorified in us when we are most satisfied in Him."[1] Our joy and God's glory are not at cross-purposes. Understood rightly, they are complementary. God would have us find our greatest joy pursuing him and his kingdom (e.g. Pss 16, 84; Matt 5:2-12).

Starting with the creature, God's pursuit of his own glory appears diabolical. Starting with God, God's pursuit of his own glory should be our greatest delight! If we are to understand God and his world, we need to begin with God and his revelation. God, not humanity, is the ultimate reference point for meaning. I suggested that for the topic of God's pursuit of his own glory, seeing God as the reference point of meaning gives us some clarity.

However, there remains much that is hidden about God's ways. Some of us may still struggle with this or another truth in God's revelation or we may encounter unanswered questions that trouble us. There comes a point in our thinking, in our pursuit of knowledge in submission to God, that we need to confess our finitude.

B. We Must Pursue Knowledge in Humility

If God is our Creator and if we are his creatures, it is obvious that he has not shared with us all of his knowledge. He knows things that we do not know. In Deuteronomy 29:29 Moses writes, "The secret things belong to the Lord our God, but the things that are revealed belong to us and to our children forever, that we may do all the words of this law." The emphasis in this passage is on God's revelation, on the Law he has revealed, yet there are

---

[1] John Piper, *Desiring God: Meditations of a Christian Hedonist*, Rev. Ed. (Colorado Springs: Multnomah, 2011), 288.

"secret things" that he has not chosen to make known. If our thinking does not have space for our finitude, we will be sorely disappointed to discover that God has not given us all his secrets.

At times we will pursue something and not find an answer. At times Biblical characters move into presumption when they reach these boundaries of human knowledge, and they dare question or challenge God. The response they receive is one we need to hear clearly today:

> But YHWH is in his holy temple;
> > be silent before him all the earth! (Hab 2:20)

> Who is this that darkens counsel by words without knowledge?
> Dress for action like a man;
> > I will question you, and you make it known to me.

> Where were you when I laid the foundation of the earth?
> > Tell me, if you have understanding.
> Who determined its measurements—surely you know!
> > Or who stretched the line upon it?
> On what were its bases sunk,
> > or who laid its cornerstone,
> when the morning stars sang together
> > and all the sons of God shouted for joy?

> Or who shut in the sea with doors
> > when it burst out from the womb,
> when I made clouds its garment
> > and thick darkness its swaddling band,
> and prescribed limits for it
> > and set bars and doors,
> and said, 'Thus far shall you come, and no farther,
> > and here shall your proud waves be stayed'?

> Have you commanded the morning since your days began,
> > and caused the dawn to know its place? (Job 38:2-12)

You will say to me then, "Why does he still find fault? For who can resist his will?" But who are you, O man, to answer back to God? Will what is molded say to its molder, "Why have you made me like this?" (Rom. 9:19-20)

By God's grace, we can know the truth! But the secret things still belong to

God. In our practical pursuit of knowing, our foundational posture must be that of humility. We must look to Yahweh to define our world, to tell us what love, righteousness, goodness, justice, peace, etc. mean. And, ultimately, we must accept—even delight in—our limitations as creatures. It is not our burden to know everything; God knows everything, and he has shared some of this with us and our children.

Further Reading

John Calvin, *The Institutes of the Christian Religion*, Book 1, Chapter 1. [B-I]
John Frame, *The Doctrine of the Knowledge of God* [I]
John Piper, *Desiring God* [B]

9

CREATED WITH SENSES: EMPIRICAL KNOWLEDGE

> That which was from the beginning, which we have heard, which we have seen with our eyes, which we looked upon and have touched with our hands, concerning the word of life—the life was made manifest, and we have seen it, and testify to it and proclaim to you the eternal life, which was with the Father and was made manifest to us—that which we have seen and heard we proclaim also to you, so that you too may have fellowship with us; and indeed our fellowship is with the Father and with his Son Jesus Christ. – 1 John 1:1-3

Throughout the history of Western thought, few things have been disparaged as much as sense knowledge. As we saw in the first chapter, the early philosopher quickly gave up on the world of the senses and turned to the mind for knowledge. The world of the senses simply changed too much. Even the so-called empiricist philosophers, who claimed that knowledge came through our senses, often maintained that the objects we sense do not actually matter. This was the case with Aristotle. Sense experience only helps us understand the abstract truths that are the true objects of knowledge.

In more recent times, philosophers have argued that we have no access to anything outside of our minds: we cannot be sure that our perceptions and experience have any correspondence with a world beyond our thoughts! Science relies on the data of the senses and interactions with the world outside of our selves. However, this is often done in naivete. Those who practice science often do so without a good reason to trust their senses, to believe that what they perceive is actually the way things are. But Christians do not have to give in to such scepticism! Indeed, God has revealed to us that our senses are a gift from him.

A. The Biblical Affirmation of the Senses

In the Christian **worldview**, human senses—such as sight and hearing—play an essential role in knowledge. Because the foundational authority for a Christian is God who has spoken, it is necessary to affirm that we can accurately perceive his speech. More than this, Yahweh is also a God who has acted and acts today and expects an appropriate response from his creatures (cf. Exod 9:16, 15:1-21).

For this to be the case, we need to be able to affirm that our senses, at their best, are trustworthy mediators of the outside world. The fact that God has entrusted us with the Bible, a written book and entrusted ministers of the Gospel to teach his word verbally assumes that our senses are trustworthy—that we can really read and hear. This is affirmed throughout the Bible. I opened this chapter with the opening words of 1 John because John is addressing a very similar question there. Instead of doubting the trustworthiness of the senses, John's readers apparently doubted the physicality—the sense-ability—of Jesus.

To affirm that Jesus Christ was indeed a physical human being as well as fully God, John appeals to the experience he and the other apostles had. He testifies to the Gospel encountered in and heard from Jesus Christ, a word that "we have heard, which we have seen with our eyes, which we looked upon and have touched with our hands" (1 John 1:1). Because we have a word from outside ourselves, a word from an authority—the one who formed us, breathed life into us, and orders our steps—we are able to affirm the reliability of the senses with which we were created. Surely the one who formed us knows the capacities of those he has formed! Yet, when this presupposition is abandoned—when an external authority is rejected—the historical rejection of the senses makes some sense.

B. The Problem with the Senses

Throughout this book, I have raised the problems non-Christians views have encountered with the senses. If we begin with our self as the authority, it becomes quickly apparent that it is impossible to prove the reliability of the senses. Reason alone cannot confirm the reliability of our senses and any appeal to sense data assumes **a priori**—before the fact—that they are reliable! Many assume without reason that their senses are reliable, but this is, of course, an irrational assumption: it has no foundation. Once you add in the fact that our senses are limited in what they encounter (i.e. we only experience an infinitesimally small part of the universe in our lifetime) the potential of the senses as a source of knowledge dwindles quickly.

To add salt to the wound, there is also the factor of psychological susceptibility: our senses are prone to deception! Walking down a sidewalk on a scorching day, we may just see pools of water on the path in front of us. Eat the wrong substance and we might hear voices others do not hear or see creatures that do not exist outside of our minds. There is also psychological illness, such as schizophrenia, that adds to the confusion of our senses! Taken together, the case against the senses seems firm: we cannot prove their reliability, we know they are deceivable, and—even if we could trust them—they do not experience enough of the world to ground our knowledge!

This is bad enough, but human reason does not get much farther (see Part 1). Even some who have claimed Christ have rejected the senses and have turned to their own minds to find certain knowledge. The problem here is that to trust our minds, we have to presuppose that all the knowledge we need to know is already known by us. For the non-Christian, this view is unacceptable; they must ask from where this knowledge came. For the Christian, this view is equally unacceptable. We are told in Scripture that our minds are hostile to the truth and ambiguous (cf. Rom 2:15; 8:6-8; Eph 4:18). More so, we are told that the knowledge of God comes through the created world and Scripture (e.g. Rom 1:20) and that God has given Scripture—not our minds alone—to equip us for every good work (2 Tim 3:16-17). As I have argued throughout this book, Christian knowledge is a combination of mental activity plus sense data, objects plus a subject interpreting them. And this, the subjective interpretation of objects, is accountable to an external authority, the mind of God revealed to his creatures.

We must, therefore, affirm that the human senses are trustworthy and necessary for knowledge. I have suggested in previous chapters that there is no knowledge without interpretation—that there is no perception without a mind interpreting it. The opposite also holds true; there is no interpretation without an object interpreted.[1] Against the objection that our senses are deceivable, we can respond that the evidence of some deception is not evidence that we are always and entirely deceived. Indeed, the fact that we identify some sensory experiences as "deception" indicates that we have normal experience against which we measure these anomalies. We interpret a mirage as such because we know what a real puddle of water is like, and we know the circumstances in which mirages happen, so we expect them.

This last point is an important one: our senses act according to consistent patterns that allow us or those outside of us to identify distortion or deception. For example, I know when I place a stick in water that the properties of water will distort the size, shape, and location of the stick. However, God has given our minds the capacity to compensate for this distortion; we are still able to retrieve the stick without a problem and are not shocked to discover that it does not appear exactly as it did underwater.[2] We also know to expect that imbibing alcohol to a certain degree or taking hallucinogenic drugs, or stressing our bodies to a great extent, will reduce the reliability of our senses. In each of these cases, the deception our senses face is predictable.

The cases of mental illness or unpredictable mental distortion of our senses are far more complicated, but one part of a greater answer is that this distortion is caused by the self and must be answered from outside of the self. That is, if our mind is deceiving us, others will not encounter the same delusion. On Biblical presuppositions (namely, that the senses are basically reliable, others exist, and that it is necessary to trust and rely on other people) we must rely on others to guide us through our delusions. In this case, we are relying on the reliability of others' senses and their character to correct our malfunctioning senses. The same is the case for those who are born with or who acquire later in life various impairments of the senses—such as deafness or blindness. Whether it is from the senses of others or from our own, the

---

[1] This has serious ramifications for the way we answer the question, "what is knowledge?" I explore this a bit in chapter 3, in the following chapter, and in Vol. 3, *The Gift of Seeing*.

[2] This is not only an ability of humans; fishing birds have the near miraculous ability to identify a fish from several dozen meters above the water and dive to catch it!

senses and the data they produce are essential to knowledge.

C. Conclusion

As Christians, we can and must affirm the reliability of our senses. This has significant implications. First, we cannot dispense with our senses, so being an armchair theologian or philosopher is out of the question. That is, we cannot just sit at home and think our way to answers for the world's problems. We must encounter the world and the people in it and study this world in light of the Word of God if we are going to provide true and helpful answers to the problems being raised. Furthermore, when our senses malfunction, we cannot retreat to the safety of our minds or rely on ourselves but must trust others to guide us by the hand—figuratively or literally.

Second, we can and must affirm the significance of human experience, particularly the experience of the inspired authors of Scripture, for faith and knowledge. That is, we cannot retreat to an intellectually detached view of the Christian faith but must root our faith in the historical events interpreted by and reported in the Bible—events seen, heard, and touched by our predecessors.

Third, we can use the Biblical affirmation of the senses to engage with other faiths intellectually. Daily life depends on reliable senses. The sciences that have given us the computers on which we write—on which I am writing right now—or the medicine that has saved many lives, that saved my life ten years ago, also depend on the reliability of our senses. Only the revelation of the one true God gives a firm foundation for trusting the senses.

Further Reading

John Frame, *The Doctrine of the Knowledge of God* [I]
Vern Poythress, *Redeeming Science: A God-Centered Approach* [I-A]

10

CREATED WITH A MIND: RATIONAL THOUGHT AND LOGIC

> This Book of the Law shall not depart from your mouth, but you shall meditate on it day and night, so that you may be careful to do according to all that is written in it. For then you will make your way prosperous, and then you will have good success. – Joshua 1:8

> God is not man, that he should lie,
> or a son of man, that he should change his mind.
> Has he said, and will he not do it?
> Or has he spoken, and will he not fulfill it? – Numbers 23:19

Imagine a world in which our minds were not trustworthy. Imagine the paralysing fear of the illogical—what if at any moment you could be alive, dead, dismembered, transported to the centre of the sun, rich beyond earthly ambition, or racked with excruciating suffering? What if you could not trust that sitting upon your chair for work would not drop you into the depths of hell itself? What if all communication was an illusion, if these words on this page could simultaneously and irrationally communicate the essential truths of life, the recipe for my favourite pizza, or you are walking through a forest on a gloomy sunny day with a solid cheese popsicle in the hand of your favourite moose?

If you have a pulse, that was probably one of the more nonsensical paragraphs you have read. The fact that you have discerned its utter absurdity demonstrates that, to some extent, your mind is functioning. To imagine a world where our minds were utterly untrustworthy is an impossible feat; we can only do so if our minds are functioning and within the framework of a world that makes sense. This book has assumed that thinking is both possible and necessary. I have written a book, presupposing that I am capable of intelligent thought and communication and that you are capable of rational thought and interpreting my communication. The subject matter itself is thought, the foundation and nature of human knowledge and knowing. That we have made it this far is a testimony to our mental abilities, given to us by God and sustained by his Spirit.

That we are capable of thinking is hard to deny, yet it has been implicitly and explicitly rejected throughout the history of human thought (catch the irony there?). For this reason, we must affirm in closing that God has indeed made us with minds capable of intelligent thought. There is no passage in Scripture that says, "God has given you the ability to think," but it is assumed without question on every page of Scripture. For example, when God created Adam, he entrusted him with the tasks of identification (i.e. identifying what trees were to be eaten and which were not) and categorisation (i.e. naming the animals, thus identifying and differentiating them) (Gen 2:18-20). Adam was able to identify which creature would be appropriate to help him in the task he had been given, none of which were (Gen 2:20). More than this, our first parents received the commission to subdue and rule the earth as the images of God. In other words, to give God glory by imitating and acting like him in shaping and governing the created world (Gen 1:28). In all of this, thought would be required—both deliberate and automatic thought. The Bible also calls on its readers to think deeply upon its words, to discern their meaning and the appropriate response to these words (e.g. Josh 1:8). From this, I surmise that thinking is God's gift to us, created and commissioned for magnifying the glory of God through thoughtful interaction with his created world.

At times the Bible disparages forms of thinking but never thinking itself. The Bible warns throughout of thinking in a lofty manner, to think in a way that denies the creaturely status of man. To think as if one were God is sinful thinking, to which God responds,

"Who is this that darkens counsel by words without knowledge?

> Dress for action like a man;
> > I will question you, and you make it known to me.
> "Where were you when I laid the foundation of the earth?
> > Tell me, if you have understanding.
> Who determined its measurements—surely you know!
> > Or who stretched the line upon it?
> On what were its bases sunk,
> > or who laid its cornerstone,
> when the morning stars sang together
> > and all the sons of God shouted for joy? (Job 38:2-7)

Thinking, as we have seen, is a moral act, so it must be done in a certain way. To think rationally, intelligently, we must think as God created us to think, in submission to him. To do so, we need the Spirit. That is, the presupposition of *consistent,* intelligent thought is not only adequate created minds but also regenerated, submitted hearts. Before this, our rebellion leads us into ignorance, but afterwards, we are equipped through Scripture to think rightly.

This does not mean that non-Christians do not exhibit intelligent thought or that Christians are the most intelligent people. What it does mean is that where non-Christians think well and arrive at the truth, they are inconsistent with their **worldview** and inconsistent with their posture of rebellion towards God. It also means that Christians have the potential to see the world better than their non-Christian peers, if they live out their Christian presuppositions faithfully through adequate natural gifting.

I have unpacked this idea throughout this book, showing that apart from submission to God as he has revealed himself in the Bible, human thought is subject to futility. In the rest of this chapter, I want to focus in on three facets of this truth that we have not yet considered, the specific ways that the Biblical worldview enables rational thought. What I have in mind is this: 1) the faithfulness of God is the presupposition of all rational thought, 2) the Bible hedges our thinking, and this is the essential condition of competent logic, 3) and the content of our thinking is interpreted objects.

A. The Presupposition of Thought

If you recall our discussion in chapter 1, you will remember that the early philosophers were obsessed with the idea of stability. That is, they perceived the need for a stable object of thought, something behind the fluxing world of our senses. The resolution I proposed to their struggles was to identify truth with our interpretation of objects measured against the standard of God's interpretation instead of static ideas floating out beyond our minds. There is a problem here, however, for our minds are also in flux like the world of experience; our memories fade, opinions change, and our certainty waxes and wanes.

By rejecting the stability provided by eternally unchanging ideas, it may appear that we have rejected the possibility of knowledge at all. God is a person; persons change. That is, they respond to and interact with others.[1] Someone may suggest, considering this, that God's interpretation of the world might change! From another perspective, is not God free? No human being or created thing can place constraint upon God, so could he not change the true interpretation of an object or event at any time? Could he not change the laws of interpretation—laws of logic and the so-called natural laws—at any time? To answer these questions in the affirmative would be to jettison the possibility of knowledge. But if we answer them negatively, with a firm Biblical answer, we also provide a stable foundation for human thought. The answer is no, God will not—indeed, he cannot—change his interpretation of objects or reject the laws of interpretation he has established. He will not, cannot, do so because he is faithful. Therefore, it is God's faithfulness that is the presupposition of rational thought.

When we say that God is faithful, we mean that he will always keep his word—fulfil every promise—and never act in a way contrary to his character. God's faithfulness guarantees that he will not sway or change on a whim, unlike a human: "God is not man, that he should lie, or a son of man, that he should change his mind. Has he said, and will he not do it? Or has he spoken, and he will not fulfil it?" (Num 23:19). He has pre-interpreted this entire creation, created and ordained its paths, laying out a plan for how all things will interact towards the revelation of his glory through Jesus Christ (e.g. Eph 1:7-10). God has created the natural order so that we could know it and behold him through it; this is the purpose of creation, and it depends on consistency in the way the world works. Because God is faithful to his purpose and has not seen fit to change his purpose for the world, it follows that we can trust the rules of interpretation by which we interpret our

---

[1] For the qualified sense in which God "changes," see Vol. 3 *The Gift of Seeing*.

experience—such as causality. Logic itself, the rules by which we think, is merely the outworking of the implications of God's own faithfulness. The foundational law of logic is that something cannot be one thing and another at the same time and in the same way (often phrased as "A or not-A at the same time and in the same way"). This is merely a universal application of God's faithfulness within himself and wired into the created order.

God cannot be true and false, faithful and unfaithful, good or bad in the same sense and at the same time. The consistency of our experience and the consistency of our minds depend, therefore, on the faithfulness of our God. It is his unchanging character that provides the necessary presupposition of human thinking. This is our great source of hope: "Let us hold fast the confession of our hope without wavering," writes the author of Hebrews, "for he who promised is faithful" (Heb 10:23).

A problem remains, however. Earlier, we saw that empirical knowledge (sense knowledge) is futile within the non-Christian position because it requires exhaustive knowledge to know anything. This problem remains in intellectual engagement, for reason depends on sense experience to furnish it with content.

B. The Necessary Condition of Thought

> I know that you can do all things,
>> and that no purpose of yours can be thwarted.
> "Who is this that hides counsel without knowledge?"
> Therefore I have uttered what I did not understand,
>> things too wonderful for me, which I did not know.
> "Hear, and I will speak;
> I will question you, and you make it known to me."
> I had heard of you by the hearing of the ear,
>> but now my eye sees you;
> therefore I despise myself,
>> and repent in dust and ashes." - Job 42:2-6

Think of a basic syllogism—a formal logical argument:

1) Socrates is a man
2) All men are mortal
3) Therefore, Socrates is mortal

How would you know that Socrates is a man? You might read a book, or if you were his contemporary, you would make this conclusion from your experience. However, with the limited knowledge of your senses, can you be sure that there is nothing just beyond your sensible experience that would invalidate this conclusion? The second proposition (i.e. "all men are mortal") is also tenuous on the basis of empirical knowledge: have you experienced the death of all men and women throughout history? What if one or two defied death (e.g. Enoch, Elijah, Jesus)? Can you really be so sure that Socrates is not immortal? Thinking, whether in formal arguments or informal reasoning, relies on an interaction between experience and laws of thought. If experience is befouled by the lack of exhaustive knowledge—if not knowing everything means you cannot know anything—then human knowledge, derived as it is from experience and thinking, is impossible without access to certain knowledge.

I suggested earlier that because God knows all things exhaustively and has revealed himself, we can know things certainly; we can have knowledge. This is the necessary condition of human thought, access to God's infinite knowledge. We can see how God's knowledge enables true knowledge by considering what philosophers have sometimes called **limiting concepts**.

A limiting concept, an idea that entered Christian thought through Cornelius Van Til, refers to a function that propositions (simple truth statements: e.g. the block is red) take in logic and reasoning. That is, statements are limiting concepts when they serve to prevent conclusions from being reached that would otherwise be valid. Representing propositions algebraically (**A, B, C**, etc.), we could give a formula for the function of a limiting concept like this: if it seems to be the case that "**A** therefore **B**," but we know that "**C** then **not-B**"; when C is true, "**A** therefore **B**" is false. In this logical equation, **A** is a true statement (e.g. "It is wet outside") and **B** is a statement that may be true or false (e.g. "it is raining"). **C** is another statement that excludes **B** from being true (e.g. $C =$ "it is too cold to rain") and is functioning as a limiting concept. That is, at first glance **A** "It is wet outside," therefore **B** "It is raining" seems reasonable—this makes sense! Yet the presence of **C** "it is too cold to rain" causes us to revisit our initial reasoning.

Because we cannot deduce **B** from **A**, we must consider other possibilities—of which there are many (e.g. **D** "a man is spraying the sidewalk with a hose"; **E** "there is a heater melting the snow"; etc.)! The limiting concept here reveals a problem in the initial logic itself: though **B** implies **A**, **A** does not *necessarily* imply **B**.

We could think of many Biblical examples where Scriptural truths act in this way. At first, it seems logical to conclude from the facts that God is one and the Father is God that Jesus cannot be God. However, we know from the Biblical testimony that Jesus is God, the Father is God, and the Spirit is God, so we are forced to reformulate our idea of God in trinitarian terms. Or if a scientist observes certain laws about the deposition of minerals and the rocks they form, they could reason back from the patterns they observe in rocks to determine the amount of time that it may have taken for the laws they observe to form such a formation. However, if Scripture teaches that the world is significantly younger than is posited in such a conclusion and teaches that these laws have not been consistent and universal in their application (i.e. a world-wide flood needs to be considered, Genesis 6-9), then the conclusions these scientists make must be false.

Limiting concepts encourage humility in reasoning, for they may invalidate conclusions that seem otherwise right. However, they also provide an essential condition of knowledge. Let us consider the problem once again. To properly understand any one detail in a system of truth (an interpretation of reality), one needs to have a perfect understanding of the whole. To give every true statement that could possibly be said about something—for instance, the location of my laptop—I must have access to every available perspective. It is in front of me, beside my lamp, beneath the roof, at a certain longitude and latitude, a certain distance from Alpha Centauri, etc. You may respond, "it is true that I need to know all things to describe something *exhaustively*, but practically I do not need to know every way a laptop's location could be described to know where it is!" That is true enough, but what if one of those unknown details is vital to knowing the location of and being able to use the laptop?

You cannot know if this detail is critical or not because you do not know what it is. If it turns out to be relevant—even vital—you will fail in some way when you try to locate and use the laptop.

Consider this thought experiment. Imagine if aliens visited Adam and Eve on the 7th day of creation and wanted to use their knowledge of human growth to determine when the world began. They could analyse Adam perfectly and conclude that the world began 41 years, 2 months, and 9 days ago. This would appear to be a sound conclusion, yet they would be wrong. The problem, in this case, is not that they do not properly understand human growth; their problem is ignorance of the fact that God created Adam only a day ago in a fully mature adult state. That one piece of data could ruin all their otherwise perfect calculations.

To perform proper induction (i.e. empirical science: gather a set of data and reach a conclusion from it) or deduction (concluding truths from other truths via logic), certain truths are needed from which to begin and from which to cut off the fruitless exploration of possibilities. Yet, if certainty only comes through exhaustive knowledge of everything, we need these truths revealed to us from one who knows all things. Therefore, we need God's input to begin any reasoning that hopes to describe the universe rightly.

This is where limiting concepts come in: in the Christian worldview, we trust that God has told us enough to properly understand his world (to reach appropriate inductive and deductive conclusions). Yet, he has not told us everything: he has given us a good foundation from which to reason from but also the knowledge that hedges in our reason—that constrains it—and guards us against going too far in our logic. What God has told us about himself, us, and the world serves both to guide us in interpreting and to prevent us from over-interpreting: it functions as a limiting concept.

Consider the Trinity. God has given us in Scripture adequate attestation that our reasoning is trustworthy, and the law of non-contradiction is presupposed in Scripture and human reason. Foundational to the Bible is the claim of Monotheism: Yahweh alone is God; he is numerically one (Deut 6:4-5). It is an appropriate deduction from this claim to reject every claim that there is a multiplicity of gods: if there are three "gods" ("god" describing each being in the same way) then there cannot be only one god. Yet, in the New Testament, Jesus differentiates himself from the Father and the Holy Spirit (the Helper) but claims for himself the status of the unique Deity: he is Yahweh (John 8:58). We are left with what appears to be a contradiction: God is one, yet Jesus is God, the Father is God, and the Holy Spirit is God. Because the first statement, "God is numerically one" is given to us by God, it is undoubtedly true; the same can be said for "Jesus, the Father, and Holy Spirit are differentiated; they are all God, yet there is only one God." Therefore, given that this last statement is true—it is attested by Scripture—

the following argument is false:

1. There are three beings called "God"
2. If three beings are called "God," there cannot be one God alone
3. therefore, there is not one God alone.

All sorts of philosophical explanations are given for how God can be one and not-one at the same time, yet they all resolve in mystery. As Christians, our logical consistency is not grounded in an explanation of how God's oneness and his threeness are not contradictory but in the fact that God has revealed to us that these are not contradictory states. He has provided a limiting concept that prevents us from deducing contradiction from the *apparent* contradiction of the Trinity.

Ultimately, limiting concepts remind us that we are creatures and servants, not God! We do not know everything; therefore, we need God to tell us where the boundaries of our logic are. When Biblical truths function as boundaries for our logic, they are functioning as limiting concepts. Consider two other examples.

First, Arminian theologians often argue that the love of God requires him to make salvation available to all equally through prevenient grace. Yet, as I have argued in my book *Prevenient Grace*, the Bible teaches that God has not acted to save all in the same way (he has made it available to all, but has not regenerated all to receive it) and it does not teach prevenient grace.[2] The doctrines of irresistible grace and unconditional election, therefore, serve as limiting concepts, causing us to revisit our understanding of God's love and not deduce false theological conclusions from it.

Second, consider one of the arguments that could be made for the age of the universe. If light takes several billion years to travel from the edge of the universe to earth, then the universe would have to be at least that old for us to see that light, which we do. The logic is this: we know the speed of light, we can calculate the distance from the earth to the farthest point away, and we are receiving light from that most distant point, therefore the universe is at least old enough for light to travel from that point to earth—several billion years worth of distance. The logic follows, but if the Bible teaches that the

---

[2] J. Alexander Rutherford, *Prevenient Grace: An Investigation into Arminianism*, 2nd Revised Ed., Teleioeti Technical Studies 2 (Vancouver: Teleioteti, 2020).

earth and universe are relatively young (maybe 6,000-10,000 years old), then this provides a limiting concept that prevents us from drawing this conclusion—as in the case of the aliens considered above. Such a limiting concept would demand a re-evaluation of the various philosophical assumptions, pieces of data, and interpretations of that data that led to a false conclusion.

The point is this. God has given us minds that work, so we must use them; yet in doing so, we need to be aware of our limitations. Our minds are not the problem; our ignorance is the problem. We do not have exhaustive knowledge of God or the creation—we do not know all there is to know—so how can we know its parts? Praise be to God that he has given us an authoritative Word that frees us from hopeless scepticism. By building our reasoning upon the foundation of the Word of God and allowing the Word to function as a limiting concept on our thinking, we can appropriately use our minds to understand better the glorious complexity of God's creation, his Word, and God himself. By giving us insight into the created world from one who knows all things, the Bible provides us with the necessary condition for the proper use of our minds.

C. The Content of Thought

This leaves us with one last loose end I think I need to tie up. In much of Western philosophy, it has been believed that the object and content of knowledge—the things we actually know—are **abstract** ideas. Abstract ideas are categories that encompass particular objects, actions, or events. Fido is a particular object, "dog" is a category. An abstract idea would be *dogness*, the essential element possessed by Fido which qualifies him as a "dog." "Dogness" as an abstract idea could be defined as "that without which something is not a dog." That is vague, but that is about as clear as philosophy gets about abstract ideas. The abstract idea *dogness* does not refer to any physical feature of a specific dog (such as tall, short, four legs, tail, brown, spotted, etc.), for we can think of dogs with or without any of these features (e.g. my neighbour has a three-legged dog). The more abstract an idea, the less it is clear what it is; we can make some sense of *dogness*, but what about *life*? If life encompasses plants, insects, men and women, cats and dogs, what content does this idea have? Throughout Western thought, it was thought that abstract ideas—called **universals**, forms, etc.—were the true objects of knowledge. However, I have defined knowledge in such a way that rules out abstraction in this sense.

a. Concrete Thought

That is, if our knowledge is an interpretation of objects, then knowledge is not abstract: it is always involved with the particular objects of our experience. Knowledge is an interaction with the created order and the Creator (particular or concrete objects) through the interpretive framework he has given us. Therefore, our knowledge is not abstract in this non-Christian sense but, to some extent, concrete. For example, consider "dog"; we do not think of abstract "dogness" when we think of "dog," we think of particular dogs and their relationship to us. We think of the cute dog on the street, the childhood dog we grew up with, or our wife's dream dog. When we think of "love" (a different kind of abstract idea) we do not think of an abstract definition of love; instead, we think of concrete examples of love we have experienced and received. Indeed, as Christians, we think of God and the love he has shown us through Jesus Christ on the cross. Historical events, present experiences, future hopes, these are the content of "love."

Yet, it should be evident that the content of our knowledge is not concrete objects themselves. Jesus Christ, Pugimus Maximus the 3rd, Fido, or the crucifixion do not exist in our minds. Instead, as we saw earlier, what is in our minds—the content of our thoughts—is a particular interpretation of these things. So, in one sense, we can say (over against the classic Western philosophical tradition) that the content of knowledge is not abstract ideas but interpretations of concrete objects—people, events, things, etc. Yet part of thinking is still abstract in some sense. We can talk about the crucifixion but also of God's *love* shown in the crucifixion. We can think about Fido but also *dogs* in general. We use abstract categories all the time, whether they are adjectives (smallness, tallness), categories (humanity), or abstract nouns (love, goodness, evil). If abstract thought is not non-Christian abstraction, we need to offer an alternative explanation.

b. Abstract Thought

I would define abstract thought as "a relationship identified between particular objects of our experience (e.g. between specific dogs, trees, persons, events, or actions) that allows us to understand other particular objects of our experience better."[3] These relationships are not objects themselves, but bridges that allow us to move from one object of our experience to another object in order to come to an understanding of the latter and enrich our understanding of both. For example, having knowledge of several dogs—Fido the poodle, Pugimus Maximus the pug, and Wolf the husky—would allow us to identify and understand a new dog that walks by us on the street. On the other hand, encountering a Pomeranian would shed further light on the variety and features that are displayed by dogs, maybe even revealing something new about one of the original objects of our knowledge. Consider the abstract term "love":

> What is it that we think of when we think of "love" or "goodness"? As much as it is not an abstract definition we think of, we also do not think of isolated events with no relation. Instead, we think of a series of events that we deem exemplary of "love." If love is neither a floating abstract definition that lays behind these events nor a random assortment of events, what remains is that "love" is a relationship between these events. Love describes a particular feature of these events that is drawn out when they are viewed in relationship with one another. It is not a "part" of these events, as if you could take an instance of me saying "I love you" to Nicole and dissect it into parts—it is part speech, love, communication, respect, etc. Instead, love describes one way of looking at this event as it shares commonality with other similar events; it is a perspective by which all these events can be viewed.[4]

As I have argued above, such a view of knowledge means that no human can attain exhaustive knowledge of the universe, as the philosophers sought. It also implies that we cannot have knowledge of anything from reason alone. Only as we use reason to interpret our experience in submission to God do we have knowledge.

---

[3] This section is derived from two articles I wrote on Teleioteti and my book *The Gift of Seeing*. This quote is taken from the article "What is Abstraction? – Part 2." https://teleioteti.ca/2018/09/20/what-is-abstraction-part-2/. See further, Vol. 3, *The Gift of Seeing*.

[4] ibid.

D. Conclusion

As Christians we must affirm the competence of the human mind to interpret the world. We must affirm the value of rational thinking and make an effort the think seriously and intelligently about our world. This starts with meditating on the Word of God but cannot be restricted to it; we must also reflect on how the Scriptures shape us and our response to the world in which we live. The existence of Yahweh and his revelation in the created order and Scripture is the presupposition of intelligent thought.

That we find much that is true and good in the non-Christian world is a testimony to the influence Christianity has had on the Western world and to the fact that no human being suppresses the knowledge of God perfectly— to do so would destroy all hope of knowing anything. Beginning from the Bible as the foundation of thought, we can have confidence in our capacities to think and interpret the world. But, despite this confidence, we must always bear great humility knowing that no matter how much insight we attain, this is only by the grace of God and represents only a minute fraction of his unfathomable knowledge.

Further Reading

*John Frame, *Apologetics: A Justification of Christian Belief* [B]
*John Frame, *The Doctrine of the Knowledge of God* [I]
John Frame, *Cornelius Van Til: An Analysis of His Thought* [I-A]
*John Piper, *Think* [B]
Very Poythress, *Logic: A God-Centered Approach to the Foundation of Western Thought* [I-A]
Vern Poythress, *Symphonic Theology: The Validity of Multiple Perspectives in Theology* [I-A]

CONCLUSION

> For consider your calling, brothers: not many of you were wise according to worldly standards, not many were powerful, not many were of noble birth. But God chose what is foolish in the world to shame the wise; God chose what is weak in the world to shame the strong; God chose what is low and despised in the world, even things that are not, to bring to nothing things that are, so that no human being might boast in the presence of God. And because of him you are in Christ Jesus, who became to us wisdom from God, righteousness and sanctification and redemption, so that, as it is written, "Let the one who boasts, boast in the Lord." – 1 Corinthians 1:26-31

The world in which we live is in the thralls of epistemological chaos—everything is backward, sideward, forwards, up and down! There is no anchor holding us firm in the foaming waves, so we are "tossed to and fro by the waves and carried about by every wind of doctrine, by human cunning, craftiness in deceitful schemes" (Eph 4:14). We see the effects of this chaos in social media, politics, newspapers, popular books, classrooms, and universities. Yet, unlike our neighbours, Christians are not left without an anchor when the waves crash around us. We do not have to be dragged along in the stream of our culture nor surrender to the nihilism that has characterized the last two centuries.

God has not left us without a witness, he has spoken. In that act of speaking, revealing himself, he has provided us with a firm foundation to withstand all the storms the threaten to submerge our nations. Instead of leaving us in the dark, captive to Kingdom of Satan expressed through the world in rebellion against God, he has entered this created order to transfer all those who believe in his Son from the kingdom of darkness into the kingdom of his glorious light.

Initially, through the Spirit, he has shone "in our hearts to give us the light of the knowledge of the glory of God in face of Jesus Christ" (2 Cor 4:6). Through Jesus Christ, God the Father has brought to fulfillment his plan to reconcile sinners to himself through the cross. By pouring out the punishment we deserved upon Jesus in our place, he has purchased for us salvation from our sins and has enacted a new **covenant** through which we receive all of his promises, in part now but fully in the age to come. This reconciliation, this beautiful gift of salvation, is hard to believe—it is foolishness to us when we were perishing (1 Cor 1:18-31). But through the Spirit he illumines our hearts to believe in and receive the salvation provided by his Son.

When we believe in the Son, he opens our eyes to perceive his glory in Scripture and the created order. For the first time, as the veil of hard hearted rebellion is removed, we begin to see the world truly, as the theatre of the glory of God. Through those who teach us, through pastors and peers, we receive a foundation from which we are able to begin interpreting the Word of God and his world correctly—as he intends. With this firm foundation, we have the promise that we can live faithfully before God in this world, that we can see the world and learn how God would have us respond to it.

For the Christian, God's gift of knowing has endless implications. To name a few, first, we need to submit ourselves to Scripture as God's authoritative revelation. Only if God has revealed himself clearly, accurately, authoritatively do we have hope to navigate the chaos of our world. God has revealed himself in this way and it is our job to grow in our knowledge of God and his world through the Word, the means he has ordained for doing so.

Second, we need to reevaluate our assumptions. It is not safe to assume that disciplines formulated within a secular worldview will be sufficient to know and respond truly to God's world. We must ask difficult questions like, how does the truth of the Word of God change the methods and conclusions of the physical sciences? How does the revelation of God change the way we do linguistics, economics, or sociology? How does the standard of the word of God shape our political opinions? How does the Biblical revelation, especially a Biblical anthropology, shape the way we understand psychology and do counselling?

Third, we need to conduct ourselves with great humility. I think I have shown that the Bible reveals to us that we can have certainty in this life. We can have final conclusions, solid opinions, firm knowledge. Yet the cost of attaining this is total submission to God! We must submit our thinking, feeling, and acting to God if we are to attain such knowledge. This is a life-long goal, pursuing sanctification through work of the Spirit. As we pursue conformity to Christ, we will find ourselves moving from the complete confidence in God's work for us through Christ to ever deepening confidence in our knowledge of his will and may even achieve a level of certainty about more speculative areas of Biblical application—such as philosophy. The knowledge we have, certainty we attain, is not based on our abilities or efforts but solely on the grace of God who shone light into the darkness of our hearts;

> consider your calling, brothers: not many of you were wise according to worldly standards, not many were powerful, not many were of noble birth. But God chose what is foolish in the world to shame the wise; God chose what is weak in the world to shame the strong; God chose what is low and despised in the world, even things that are not, to bring to nothing things that are, so that no human being might boast in the presence of God. And because of him you are in Christ Jesus, who became to us wisdom from God, righteousness and sanctification and redemption, so that, as it is written, "Let the one who boasts, boast in the Lord." (1 Cor 1:26-30)

For the Christian, then, the application is this: read the Scriptures and know God; read the Scriptures and believe God; read the Scripture and live for God in this world. Make known his light in the darkness through the preaching of the Gospel of his risen Son, the only message that can save sinners and the only hope for the epistemologically lost.

For the unbeliever, the gift of knowing God has given his creatures begs a response. Will you continue groping around in the dark, trusting yourself or other man-made authorities for hope? To do so will only result in hopeless nihilism now and eternal judgment when Christ returns. Yahweh is the creator of this world and apart from him, there is no hope to understand and live in it. Indeed, to seek to live apart from him is to engage in rebellion against him, to reject the Creator and worship the creature. We all worship something. The question is, will we worship the Creator or another god—sex, drugs, money, respectability, influence, power, etc. To worship another, a false god, is to invest your hope in nothing—a fleeting shadow—and invite the judgment of the one true God.

To worship the Yahweh is to cast yourself on his mercy, to repent of rebellion and trust in the life, death, and resurrection of his Son for salvation. To cast ourselves on the mercy of God costs everything—our independence, even our very life—but gains for us far more than we lost (Matt 10:39, John 12:25) . Not only are we delivered from the wrath of God against sin, but we enter his family, expressed in the local church, and inherit the purpose of magnifying his name throughout the earth. And at his return, we inherit joy everlasting in the presence of God in a new creation—a new heaven and earth free from sin, rebellion, death, and pain. This is the hope of all who believe: life and joy now through the Spirit of God among his people and life and joy forevermore in the presence of the Triune God in a new creation. This hope is life, not death; purpose, not nihilism; hope, not despair; and truth, not a lie. These are the promises of God for those who cast themselves upon his mercy and delight in the things he has revealed.

> The secret things belong to the LORD our God, but the things that are revealed belong to us and to our children forever, that we may do all the words of this law. (Deut 29:29)

GLOSSARY

Abstraction

In this book, and in several other works of mine, I offer a different view of abstraction than the standard non-Christian view. There are, therefore, at least two different ways we may define abstraction. For the non-Christian, an abstraction is an idea or generalization (animal – mammal – humanity) of related particulars (Bill, Bob, Jane, Judy). It also refers to the process of moving from particular objects (a specific rock, person, tree, or dog) to generalized categories (humanity, dogs, inanimate objects, being) or properties (red, green; largeness, smallness). In other words, moving from sensible (concrete) objects or events to mental (abstract) ideas.

I contend above that a more biblical view of abstraction is a relationship identified between particular objects of our experience (e.g. a specific dog, tree, person) that allows us to understand other particular objects of our experience better. It also refers to "the process of identifying similarities among particular objects." In other words, abstraction is the identification of a relationship between objects of our experience. See pgs. 636-651, 681-683.

Apologetics

Apologetics can be considered as the attempt to present or defend the Christian faith in a persuasive and intellectual manner. That is, apologetics aims to be *persuasive*, to make an argument in order to convince another. It does not merely state the truth but argue for and defend it. Particularly, apologetics is an intellectual endeavour because it attempts to reason with others and persuade them about truth. John Frame defines apologetics as *"the discipline that teaches Christians how to give a reason for their hope."* He identifies three aspects in this, proof "presenting a rational basis for faith" (John 14:11, 20:24-31; 1 Cor 15:1-11); defence, "answering the objections of unbelief (e.g. Phil 1:7); and offence, "attacking the foolishness of unbelieving thought (Ps 14:1; 1 Cor 1:18-2:16).[1]

A Priori

In philosophy, *a priori* is used in a particular way: something is *a priori* when it is believed apart from sense experience. It could then refer to innate knowledge—knowledge we have from birth—or logically deduced knowledge.[2]

A Posteriori

A posteriori is the opposite of *a priori*; knowledge is *a posteriori* when it is derived from sense experience. Neither innate ideas or knowledge deduced from rationally derived propositions is *a posteriori*, but the knowledge derived from the senses and logical deductions from sense data are *a posteriori* knowledge.

Covenant

A covenant, in the Bible, is a formalized relationship between two groups that involves mutual commitments—promises made to one another—and, often, serious consequences for breaking those commitments. God's relationship with humans is consistently covenantal.

Empiricism

Empiricism is the philosophical position that knowledge is derived from the senses and not from reason alone. Empiricists are not necessarily concerned with particular objects of experience, for experience is often seen as the way to arrive at **abstract** truth (as in Aristotle, for example). Empiricists nevertheless value the senses and are interested in gaining and analysing experience.

---

[1] *Apologetics: A Justification of Christian Belief*, (P&R, 2015), 1-2.
[2] This definition, and several of those that follow, are based on the glossaries of my book *Prevenient Grace* (Teleioteti, 2020) and my thesis *God's Kingdom Through His Priest-King* (ThM, Regent College, 2018).

Epistemology

Epistemology is a 50-dollar philosophical word used to describe the study of knowledge and knowing. Epistemology addresses what we think and how we think it, what truth means and how we can find it—if we can at all. It is one of the three traditional divisions of philosophy—metaphysics, epistemology, and ethics.

Foundationalism

Foundationalism is a modernist epistemology, a view of knowing that emerged after the enlightenment. Foundationalism claims to be able to prove certain self-evident truths, or axioms, and then tries to establish all human knowledge on the basis of this foundation. Narrow foundationalists based everything on one or two axioms, as was the case with Descartes, but broad foundationalists base everything on a larger body of evident truths, such as the Christian philosophers Alvin Plantinga and Ronald Nash.

Postmodern philosophy has rightly rejected foundationalist theories of epistemology. Narrow foundationalism fails to move past the self as its starting point; broad foundationalism fails to be persuasive and worldviews based upon it do not provide a robust enough response to the pluralism of our day. They are ultimately not successful in showing how they are the truth over against competing worldviews. Furthermore, neither broad nor narrow foundationalism locates ultimate authority in God and His revelation.[3]

Immanence

"Immanence" is another keyword in philosophy and theology. Like transcendence, it is also a spatial term: it refers to something near at hand, close by. God's immanence is his presence with humanity. The radical immanence of Modernity refers to the belief that all truth and standards of truth lay in human beings, not in a distant idea or a supreme God.

Innate Ideas

Innate ideas are ideas that we do not and cannot learn from experience, for

---

[3] For more on foundationalism, see my review of J. P. Moreland's *Scientism and Secularism*, https://teleioteti.ca/2018/11/07/review-of-scientism-and-secularism/.

experience requires them. They are, therefore, **a priori** not **a posteriori** ideas. They differ from other *a priori* knowledge in that they are the basic ideas with which reason works; they are not the products of reason. Innate ideas in Western philosophy are **abstract ideas**, generalizations that give meaning to the objects of our experience.

In this book, I have used innate ideas in a slightly different way. Instead of viewing innate ideas as abstract ideas in the traditional sense, true knowledge waiting to be discovered, I have defined innate ideas as the interpretative categories necessary to make knowledge out of our sense experience. We are hardwired by God, for example, to recognize a pattern of relationship between different events that we call in English "love" and associate this idea with the character of God. Innate ideas are essential to human knowing; this is most clearly seen in the case of the **law the non-contradiction**. However, because of the fall, humans have suppressed these innate ideas—this tacit worldview—and need the Bible to re-form the proper interpretative lens.

Barring disability, we are also born with the concepts necessary to interpret light as different colours and to interpret this light in order to produce a mental picture.

Law of Non-Contradiction

The law of non-contradiction, an **innate idea** that is the **presupposition** of all rational thought, is the principle that no object or idea can be itself and its opposite at the same time in the same way. For example, the letter A cannot be whatever is not-A at the same time, nor can 2+3 = 5 and 6 at the same time and in the same way. A computer cannot be fully black and fully white in the same way and at the same time, though it could have a fully black layer on top of a fully white one. A phone cannot be totally unbroken and totally broken simultaneously. Such examples could be multiplied endlessly. It often summarized like this: nothing can be A and not-A at the same time in the same way. "A" is a placeholder for any attribute or state given to an object (black and not-black) or idea (true and not-true).

Without this law, learning is impossible: though I burned my hand on the stove once, it is possible that I could not burn it in these exact circumstances. Furthermore, all thought is nonsense: I could be black and white, male and female, up and down, left and right, bee or bird, human or monkey, in space or on earth, this or that, at any time and in any way.[4]

Objectivism

Objectivism is the belief that truth is out there—beyond our minds—to be grasped. Because truth is external to minds, is objective, it would be the same no matter who thought about it. Objectivity is a key concept of Modernity.

To be objective is to be neutral, to be free from bias: if truth is objective and is attained through objective thinking, it is the same no matter who is thinking it. No matter who runs the test, not only should the results be the same but their interpretation as well. Is, for example, a rock red if no one observes that it is red? If so, then "the rock is red" is objective truth, but if "the rock is red" is only true when someone observes that it is red, then it is **subjective** truth.

Objectivism is the belief that truth is outside of our minds and equally accessible to everyone. Because objectivism places truth *out there*, it implies a correspondence theory of truth. On this view, a belief is true if it corresponds to universally accessible, extra-mental reality. Modern objectivism places the "objective reality" in the **empirical** world of our senses. Pre-modern, Platonic objectivism places this objective reality in the world of the forms, a **transcendent** non-material realm.

Presupposition

A presupposition is one of our foundational beliefs by which we automatically—without deliberate thought—interpret all our experience and from which we do all our reasoning. They are someone's most base heart commitments, those beliefs that play a key role in all their reasoning and which are held with most certainty.

Subjectivism

Subjectivism is the opposite of objectivism; it is the belief that truth is dependent on the interpreter. In some forms of subjectivism, the reality of

---

[4] If the statements "J. Alexander Rutherford is floating in space, not on earth, at 10:30 am, Nov. 11, 2017" and "J. Alexander Rutherford is on earth, not in space, at 10:30 am, Nov. 11, 2017" are both true, than any contradictory state can be true (e.g. it is only snowing and only not-snowing at the same time in the same place).

an extra-mental world is denied (anti-realism). In others, an external world is affirmed but truth and knowledge are wholly dependent on the mind of the subject. In these strong forms, the inevitable implication of subjectivism is relativism; you and I can believe two mutually exclusive ideas and have mutually exclusive interpretations of the same reality—or you may not even exist.

The epistemology I present in this book is partly subjectivist but also partly objectivist. With the subjectivists, I claim that there is no knowledge or truth apart from the interpreting subject. However, with objectivist I argue that this interpretation is based on an extra-mental reality and can be right or wrong. The two views are mediated by truth that God is the first and absolute interpreter of all reality. He has granted us the ability to interpret the world correctly, as he has created and interpreted it, if we submit ourselves to him and look at the world through His lens. This means there are three interrelated aspects in human knowledge; a knowing subject, an object known, and God's interpretation to which truth will correspond and falsehood will deviate.[5]

Transcendence

Transcendence is a key idea in philosophy and theology, describing that which is other than man, that which is far off or different. It is basically a spatial concept, referring to something above us, "up there," but in philosophy or theology it refers to the quality of being greater than and so exercising control over. The universal ideas are greater than human thoughts, human ideas. They are the true content of human thinking and so exercise control over it.

Universal

Universals can be a difficult concept to wrap our minds around. A universal, for Plato, referred not to specific objects, such as a particular tree, but ideal or abstract conceptions of objects, such as the perfect "tree." By definition, such a tree could not physically exist—it could not exist in the sensible world—so it could only be an idea, a sort of template by which all other trees

---

[5] As should be evident from the recommended reading, this view is highly dependent on the work of John Frame, especially his book *The Doctrine of the Knowledge of God*.

take their features.

In one illustration, Plato pictured the relationship of universal (treeness) and particular (a tree) with a jar and its shadow. As light shines on a jar and casts a rough copy of it on the wall behind, so the idea of something creates imperfect representations of itself in the material world. In morality, there is the idea of "goodness"; every good act is an imperfect example of ideal goodness.

If you are still struggling with the concept of universals, take comfort. I think these "universals" ultimately do not make sense and are false. You cannot imagine "goodness" apart from good acts because it does not exist apart from them; the same goes for humanness, being, etc. See chapter 10.

Worldview

A worldview is essentially the interpretive framework, or the glasses, through which we view the world. That is, all of us look at the world with "rose-coloured glasses": none of us see it without interpreting it. This interpretation comes from our worldview: I recognize a tree as a God's handiwork and praise him because he created it. An atheist thinks it is a testimony to evolution and wonders at the marvellous fact that something so intricate happens to exist. We have looked at worldviews throughout this book, especially in Volume 1, Chapter 2, and in Volume 3. We can define it as a comprehensive framework for interpreting and making decisions.

The term "worldview" often refers to that aspect of our interpretive framework that can be expressed in propositional statements. In this sense, a worldview is the sum-total of ones most basic beliefs, or presuppositions, about the nature of the world, knowledge, ethics, life's purpose, etc. James N. Anderson helpfully summarises the major beliefs of a worldview in this sense as TAKES, as in "what it TAKES to make a worldview." *Theology*, what is the absolute (God or alternate explanation of everything) in your worldview? *Anthropology*, what do you believe about man? *Knowledge*, what is truth and how do we get it? *Ethics*, what is right or wrong, good or bad? And *Salvation*, what is the problem with the world and how is it fixed? However, as we saw, this is merely the tip of the iceberg: worldviews also involve conceptual and person knowledge, which cannot be expressed in propositions and which function at a tacit level (see further, Volume 3).

The Gift of Knowing

BIBLIOGRAPHY

Bahnsen, Greg L. *Van Til's Apologetic: Readings and Analysis.* Phillipsburg: P&R Publishing, 1998.

Calvin, John. *Institutes of the Christian Religion.* Translated by Henry Beveridge. Peabody, Mass: Hendrickson Publishers, 2008.

Chamberlain, Paul. *Can We Be Good without God? A Conversation about Truth, Morality, Culture & a Few Other Things That Matter.* Downers Grove: InterVarsity Press, 1996.

Craig, William Lane. *On Guard: Defending Your Faith With Reason And Precision.* Colorado Springs, Colo.: David C. Cook, 2010.

———. *The Kalam Cosmological Argument.* Eugene, OR: Wipf and Stock Publishers, 2000.

Frame, John. "'Infinite Series.'" *Frame-Poythress.Org.* Last modified May 21, 2012. Accessed July 28, 2021. https://frame-poythress.org/infinite-series/.

Frame, John M. *A History of Western Philosophy and Theology.* Phillipsburg: P&R Publishing, 2015.

———. *Apologetics: A Justification of Christian Belief.* Edited by Joseph E. Torres. Second edition. Phillipsburg, New Jersey: P&R Publishing, 2015.

———. *Cornelius Van Til: An Analysis of His Thought*. Phillipsburg: P&R Publishing, 1995.

———. *Systematic Theology: An Introduction to Christian Belief*. Phillipsburg: P&R Publishing, 2013.

———. *The Doctrine of the Knowledge of God*. A Theology of Lordship. Phillipsburg: P&R Publishing, 1987.

———. *The Doctrine of the Word of God*. A Theology of Lordship. Phillipsburg: P&R Publishing, 2010.

Grudem, Wayne. *Systematic Theology: An Introduction to Biblical Doctrine*. Leicester; Grand Rapids: Inter-Varsity Press ; Zondervan, 1994.

Hume, David. *Dialogues Concerning Natural Religion*. Dover Philosophical Classics. Mineola, N.Y.: Dover Publications, 2006.

Lewis, C. S. *Miracles: A Preliminary Study*. New York: Harper Collins, 2011.

Long, V. Philips. "The Art of Biblical History." In *Foundations of Contemporary Interpretation*, edited by Moisés Silva. Grand Rapids: Zondervan, 1996.

Luther, Martin. *The Bondage of the Will*. Edited by J. I Packer and O. R Johnston. Grand Rapids: Fleming H. Revell, 2003.

Moreland, James Porter. *Scientism and Secularism: Learning to Respond to a Dangerous Ideology*. Wheaton: Crossway, 2018.

Nash, Ronald H. *Worldviews in Conflict : Choosing Christianity in a World of Ideas*. Grand Rapids: Zondervan, 1992.

Nietzsche, Friedrich Wilhelm, and Walter Kaufmann. *The Portable Nietzsche*. New York, N.Y.: Penguin Books, 1982.

Piper, John. *A Peculiar Glory: How the Christian Scriptures Reveal Their Complete Truthfulness*. Wheaton: Crossway, 2016.

———. *Desiring God: Meditations of a Christian Hedonist*. Rev. Ed. Colorado Springs: Multnomah, 2011.

———. *Think: The Life of the Mind and the Love of God.* Wheaton: Crossway, 2010.

Poythress, Vern S. *Logic: A God-Centered Approach to the Foundation of Western Thought.* Electronic. Wheaton: Crossway, 2013.

———. *Symphonic Theology: The Validity of Multiple Perspectives in Theology.* Grand Rapids: Academie Books, 1987.

Poythress, Vern Sheridan. *Redeeming Science: A God-Centered Approach.* Wheaton: Crossway Books, 2006.

Rutherford, J. Alexander. *Prevenient Grace: An Investigation into Arminianism.* 2nd Revised Ed. Teleioteti Technical Studies 2. Vancouver: Teleioteti, 2020.

Sagan, Carl. *The Demon-Haunted World: Science as a Candle in the Dark.* 1st Ed. New York: Ballantine Books, 1997.

Schaeffer, Francis A. *He Is There and He Is Not Silent.* Carol Stream: Tyndale House Publishers, 2013.

———. *The God Who Is There.* 30th Anniversary Ed. Downers Grove: IVP, 1998.

———. *The Great Evangelical Disaster.* Westchester: Crossway Books, 1984.

Van Til, Cornelius. *Christian Theistic Evidences.* Edited by K. Scott Oliphint. Second Edition, Including the complete text of the original 1978 edition. Phillipsburg: P&R Publishing, 2016.

———. *The Defense of the Faith.* Edited by K. Scott Oliphint. 4th ed. Phillipsburg: P & R Pub, 2008.

Warfield, Benjamin B. "Inspiration." In *Selected Shorter Writings of Benjamin B. Warfield.* Vol. 1. Phillipsburg: P & R, 2001.

The Gift of Knowing

ABOUT TELEIOTETI

Teleioteti (Τελειοτητι, te-ley-o-tey-tee)—meaning "unto maturity"—is dedicated to faithful, thoughtful ministry. We create resources for Christian discipleship, resources that address theological and pastoral concerns from a Biblical worldview. Our purpose is to see Christ's Church mature in its understanding of God and His Word. We do this through the production of Gospel-centred materials that connect the Bible with the heads, hearts, and minds of Christians. We hope to enable Christians from all walks of life to better understand and glorify God through service in His Church.

To achieve this purpose, Teleioteti publishes online materials and books researched with academic rigour yet based upon Biblical presuppositions. That is, we are neither academic nor lazy. We use methods, or epistemology, informed by the Bible along with the hard work usually associated with professional research and study. We produce resources directed towards all Christians, but most of our resources are directed towards students, pastors, and theologically inclined lay Christians.

To learn more about us and what we are doing, please visit us at https://teleioteti.ca or contact us at info@teleioteti.ca. If you have found this resource helpful, prayerfully consider supporting us by giving a review on the web (e.g. Amazon, Goodreads, etc.), praying with and for us, or giving financially so that we can produce more resources like this one. For more information on how you can support us, visit us at https://teleioteti.ca/about/partner/ or at our page on Patreon, https://www.patreon.com/teleioteti.

Other Books by J. Alexander Rutherford

Prevenient Grace: An Investigation into Arminianism – 2nd Revised Edition (Teleioteti, 2021)

When a building is built on a poor foundation, the inevitable result is its collapse. But this isn't a book on architecture; foundations are found in thought structures as well as in material structures. In theology, a bad foundation will produce results as catastrophic as a bad foundation in architecture. How we think about God and His work in the world will profoundly affect how we live and work out our Christian faith; is your foundation strong? This book evolved from the conviction that a prominent theological system rests on a fragile foundation.

Endorsements:

This book is a fine piece of scholarship. Rutherford presents his arguments with admirable clarity. His intention is to offer guidance for pastors and teachers who may be faced with questions about whether human beings have the freedom to accept or reject God. The great strength of Rutherford's book is his knowledge of Biblical texts and an appropriate interpretation of them. He successfully shows that the claims of Arminianism with its view that prevenient grace allows an acceptance or rejection of God are not supported by Biblical texts. Nor are they justified by philosophical arguments. They layout of the book and its careful treatment of arguments both for and against prevenient grace is a model of excellent writing. His chapters are supplemented by a Glossary that explains all specific terms and Appendices where detailed theological discussions are given. Most helpful is his Index of Scripture passages discussed.

- Dr. Shirley Sullivan, FRSC (elected), Professor Emeritus of Classics, University of British Columbia

Habakkuk: An Exegetical-Theological Commentary (Teleioteti, 2020)

It is all to common to find commentaries that miss the forest for the trees, commentaries that get so caught up in the minutiae of scholarly controversies that they miss what God is saying for His church today. This is especially evident when it comes to the book of Habakkuk.

The Teleioteti Old Testament Commentaries series is an attempt to attain theological depth, to pay attention to the forest, without neglecting the details of the text, without missing the trees. To do this, a Teleioteti Old Testament Commentary seeks to bring scholarly rigour and thoughfulness together with faithful attention to the purpose and significance of each book for God's people today. It strikes a balance between technicality, working through the Hebrew text and its difficulties, and practicality, applying each major section of the text to contemporary needs.

Habakkuk is a book that especially needs such an approach. After an extensive introduction discussing the significant issues and laying the groundwork for interpreting Habakkuk, this commentary walks through the text stanza by stanza and line by line. With a balance of theological reflection and exegetical depth, a wide variety of readers will find something to take away.

Habakkuk is a book of discipleship, a book written to bring its reader to a deeper faith in Yahweh in the presence of His unthinkable deeds. In the midst of oppressive evil at the hands of their Judahite brothers, the righteous of Judah cry out to God for salvation. His response is the invasion of fearsome Chaldea. What appears to be horrid judgment is actually His plan to save those who trust in Him. All His people are called to extraordinary faith, to believe Him when HIs deeds are unbelievable. In this way, and only this way, will they be delivered from their oppressors and enjoy God's blessings: only by faith can they have life.

Believe the Unbelievable: A Study in Habakkuk (Teleioteti, 2018)

What would we do if our prayers for justice, our prayers that God's will be done in our nation, were answered with a vision of desolation, of utter destruction?

When Habakkuk prayed for salvation, a prayer for justice in the midst of chaos, violence, and suffering, that was God's answer. He revealed in a vision the invasion of the vicious armies of Babylon. God's answer contradicted everything Habakkuk thought he knew. Yet in the end, he praised God and trusted Him for this horrid salvation.

What do we do when God's actions or words contradict our understanding, contradict what we have believed? The book of Habakkuk answers this question in the face of the Babylonian invasion of Judah. Habakkuk is a book of discipleship, a book written to bring its reader to a deeper faith in Yahweh in the presence of His unthinkable deeds.

Using study questions addressing the text, theology, and application of Habakkuk and explanatory comments on difficult themes, *Believe the Unbelievable* seeks to realize this purpose for the contemporary reader.

Endorsements:

James Rutherford is a capable and creative thinker, well equipped to tackle tough projects, such as the book of Habakkuk. In this study guide, Rutherford has produced a very useful resource for individual or group study. He combines theological acumen and well-honed linguistic and literary skills to discover and then to present, in highly understandable fashion, the riches of this not so "minor" Minor Prophet.

- V. Philips Long, PhD Cambridge
    Professor of Old Testament, Regent College

My good friend, James Rutherford, has given the church a gift. He has taken his love for God's Word and focused it on an Old Testament book that most Christians know very little about. The result is a study in Habakkuk that brings together deep insight and real relevance. Habakkuk is a voice among the Biblical chorus that believers need to hear today. Thank you, James, for helping us to hear it clearly and faithfully.

- Fredrick Eaton
    Pastor, Christ City Church, Kitsilano

www.ingramcontent.com/pod-product-compliance
Lightning Source LLC
Chambersburg PA
CBHW021447070526
44577CB00002B/291